D0108253

The FILM BUFF's
BUCKET LIST

The 50 movies of the 2000s
to see before you die

Theaters around the world are dominated by comic book heroes, ice princesses, apocalyptic love-struck teens, and whatever masterpiece Pixar is rolling out. It's clear that cinema is as healthy as ever. Oscar-worthy directors, indie geniuses and foreign artists are creating stunning, boundary-pushing work. Since the turn of the century, movie lovers have been enjoying a second golden age. But which films are the best of the best? What are the top movies since 2000 to see before you die? Chris Stuckmann, one of YouTube's most popular film reviewers gives us his best of the best! In his book debut, Stuckmann delivers his list of the very best 50 Movies since 2000 – with that style and punch that YouTube viewers have come to love. These are the films you must see before you die.

Dedication:

To my parents, for trying to understand my passion.
To my wife, for that push I need to pursue it.
To my friends, for inspiring me to follow it.
And to you, for actually caring.

"Chris Stuckmann is the real deal. His brain is equal parts "book smarts" and "useless movie factoids smart" – By combining both skills so beautifully he's able to offer some of the most intelligent, concise and entertaining movie a¹nalysis online. I'm a huge fan!"

Andy Signore, Founder & Creator of ScreenJunkies & Honest Trailers

"A celebration of movie love, by a lover of movies, for the lovers of movies. Equal parts fun & insightful."

Jeremy Jahns, YouTube Movie Reviews

FOREWORD

Scott Mantz
Film Critic for Access Hollywood

"Get Stuckmannized!"

Over the course of my 15-year career as the resident film critic and film correspondent for Access Hollywood, I've had many high points: interviewing Tom Cruise in Vienna in support of *Mission: Impossible– Rogue Nation*; sharing my *Star Trek* bar mitzvah photo album with Chris Pine and Zachary Quinto during the London junket for *Star Trek Into Darkness*; interviewing Ringo Starr on his 75th birthday while wearing one of my (many!) Beatles tee shirts; being recognized by Drew Barrymore, who saw my film reviews on the little TVs in the back of NYC taxis; and the chance to discover so many independent gems while covering the Sundance, Toronto and Telluride film festivals.

But, without question, the highest point of them all was when my good friend and very respected film critic Chris Stuckmann asked me to write the forward for his new book about the 50 best movies of the last 15 years.

But I'm getting ahead of myself here. I can't talk about Chris without telling my own backstory of how I became a film critic.

When I grew up in Philadelphia, movies were my passion. I was introduced to celluloid heroes at a very young age, thanks to my forward-thinking parents, who took me to see very grown-up movies like *Jaws, Taxi Driver, Rocky, Foul Play, Star Wars, The Spy Who Loved Me* and *Close Encounters of the Third Kind*.

What the hell were they thinking? *Taxi Driver*? I was 7-years-old, for cryin' out loud!

But that's where my passion for film was born. I was never much of a sports fan. I was bored to tears watching sports, and I sucked in my brief attempts to play them. It was a hard time for me, because my dad, my brother and all my friends were downright sports fanatics. I became something of a loner, so while they were watching the big games or playing two-touch football or wiffle ball in the cul-de-sac, I would ride my bike to the local theaters, where I continued my cinematic education. It was a glorious time, thanks to then-new releases like *Alien, Apocalypse Now, Raging Bull, The Empire Strikes Back, The Shining, Raiders of the Lost Ark,*

Star Trek II: The Wrath of Khan and the movie that would become my all-time favorite: *Blade Runner.*

As I grew older, my love for film knew no bounds. I saw and read everything I could about the greatest filmmakers of all time. But making a living in the movie business was something that never occurred to me. Movies were a hobby– a big hobby, but nothing more. So when it came time to choose a major while studying as an undergrad at Penn State University, I did what any clueless teenager with an accountant for a father might have done. I majored in Accounting. And I hated every friggin' minute of it.

Okay, long story short: It turned out to be a blessing in disguise, because I got a job as a financial controller at an entertainment marketing company and I moved to Los Angeles in December of 1991. After a few years there, I started writing film reviews in 1998 for a bunch of entertainment news websites that don't even exist anymore: Big Time Hollywood, Entertainment Insiders, The Mediadrome, and a few others that I really can't remember the names of.

But I found my calling, and those reviews helped me get a very good gig at Access Hollywood, where I learned the ropes as a producer while honing my skills as a film critic. It was during this time that I realized how much film critics were becoming an endangered species. While the Internet gave a voice to a lot of aspiring critics, it also put paid critics on the line, since so many up-and-comers were doing it for free. Unless critics were already established, like Roger Ebert and Peter Travers, the prospect of making a good living as a critic was becoming a thing of the past – that is, unless someone found a way to take advantage of the new online frontier while staying true to what the great critics were all about.

That's where Chris Stuckmann came in. When I first discovered his YouTube channel, which currently has more than 500,000 subscribers (and counting), I was immediately captivated by how articulate, passionate, fun, smart and entertaining his reviews were. Whether he loved a film, just sort-of liked it or downright hated it, he still spoke about it with an incredible amount of respect for the craft. His "man cave," where he shoots his reviews, is packed to the rim with movie posters, memorabilia, action figures, DVDs and Blu-rays – so, yes, it looked just like my "man cave." He was also a dashing young fellow who could give Tom Cruise a run for his money in the good-looks department.

No one else was doing what he was doing, and if they tried, they certainly weren't doing it the way he did it. I became an instant fan.

In short, I was Stuckmannized!

And as you will see in the pages that follow, he's also a damn good writer. He knows his stuff, and he writes about movies in a way that's easily accessible and extremely intelligent for both film buff and casual movie lovers. If there was ever a book about movies that qualifies as a page-turner, then the one you're holding in your hot little hands is it.

And being asked by my own favorite film critic to write the forward for his very first book (hopefully of many) was not just an honor, but also a high point of my own career. Now, as you can imagine, critics don't always see eye-to eye, and sometimes it's more fun when they don't. But I sure do agree with most of the 50 reviews you'll read here, and they're all so passionately well-written that I could feel myself getting Stuckmannized on a whole new level.

- Scott Mantz

INTRODUCTION
Chris Stuckmann
author

The screen.

Why do we go to the movies? Why do we sit in dark rooms, digging our fingers into popcorn buckets, hoping for transport to another world?

I recall watching a particularly good film earlier this year in a packed theater. I glanced about briefly and saw a couple hundred heads, all transfixed by the screen. For most, it's like peering into a parallel universe, a place where their problems don't exist. But for a very select few, it's not just about escapism, it's about searching. These people seek something more meaningful, they want to be inspired, changed, altered. They're looking for that moment when a film touches them so deeply, it's like it was playing specifically for them.

I remember that moment in my life. It was a warm Ohio day (August 2nd, 2002 to be exact). My mother and I went to a small town theater that's since been demolished. Plaza 8 at Chapel Hill. I'll never forget that place. The film my mother took me to was *Signs*, directed by M. Night Shyamalan. Since it was late summer, there was a sense that fun was winding down. School would be starting soon and I wanted to squeeze every last drop out of my summer vacation. Evidently, many others shared the same notion, because the theater was packed to near full capacity.

The lights went down, and I was instantly taken by the thrilling musical composition of James Newton Howard, instructed by Shyamalan to create a piece similar in ferocity to Bernard Hermann's opening theme for *Psycho*. The music warned me that something terrifying was coming, and the film kept its promise. In my fourteen years, I hadn't seen a film that suspenseful, and I vividly remember peeking out over the tops of my curled knees during the "disturbing footage" scene.

As a child, movies were a humongous part of my life. I wore out my *Star Wars* VHS tapes so badly that no amount of "tracking" could fix the little bouncy white lines at the bottom of the TV. But it wasn't until that warm day in the summer of '02 that I had an epiphany.

Movies were made by artists.

Directors. Writers. Actors. Editors. Cinematographers.

Movies were shot and cut together by someone. A composer wrote music to seamlessly blend with it. Someone arranged lights and objects within a shot to create visual synergy.

I have a perfect memory of returning home that day and bounding toward our apartment while saying to my mother, "I want to do that! I want to make a movie like that."

After seeing *Signs* in theaters five times, I became fascinated with filmmaking. I didn't just watch movies anymore, I studied them. The shot structure, the moment where a character reaches their arc, how a clever editor can heighten the tension with just the right cut. Everything! I lived and breathed movies. My parents must have seen a kid who'd discovered his passion, because one day, a package arrived at home containing a small camcorder. As far as I was concerned, it was the closest I'd ever get to being handed a dream, complete with bubble wrap.

The entirety of my teenage years were spent making countless short films with friends. If they weren't around, I'd even make one by myself. It didn't matter what the story was. If an idea popped into our heads, we just started filming it, sometimes without even knowing how it would end. It was blind inspiration, and a very wonderful time in my life. Of course, as we grew older, our films became more mature. One of my favorites was a tongue-in-cheek tribute to John Carpenter's *Halloween* called The Marguerite Avenue Killings. Is it strange that with a title like that, no one dies in the short?

At the same time, my love for film as an art form began to evolve, with the creation of my first website called "A Critic's Opinion." Without internet at home, the library clerk saw me quite often during those few years. Mercifully, the free hosting provider shut down its services, and my novice site vanished from the net.

No matter what, my interest in filmmaking and movies never wavered. We tried our hand at two feature-length films, and to our credit, we actually completed a 70-minute film about a magical baseball diamond called Phenomenon Field, and an 84-minute horror film called The Woods. The latter took us two years to finish, and the lessons learned while filming were worth every minute spent.

It wasn't until my early twenties that I had the idea of combining my passions. My love of film was glaringly apparent, and the hundreds of short films we'd created made my devotion to directing obvious. But I also loved analyzing film, studying the art form and trying to get in the head of the filmmaker. And, with the advent of YouTube, I suddenly had a place to express myself. My first video review was of Hayao Miyazaki's *Ponyo*. Within a month, I had a small handful of subscribers, the majority being my very patient friends.

Seven years later, I have over 500,000 subscribers, and growing. I've met count-less film enthusiasts who share my passion, and I've been deeply inspired by their personal stories of self-discovery. Without them, I have no idea where I'd be today. To my sheer delight, I've had the opportunity to meet M. Night Shyamalan, shake his hand, and thank him for inspiring me. After telling him the story I've just told you, he gave me an awestruck smile and said, "You're gonna make me cry, man."

What continues to inspire me today?

It's the screen. That glowing, shiny rectangle.

I stare at it in awe, silently willing it to show me something incredible.

* * * *

Now, I've been given the immense privilege to discuss a handful of films that meant something to me, the majority of which I've had the opportunity to see in theaters. The following fifty films released from the year 2000 to 2015 are movies that absolutely must be seen, because they were evocative of their era, they spoke to our culture, or perhaps they're overlooked gems. These films are presented in order of release date. This is not a countdown. Not only do I find lists superfluous, but this also eliminates the temptation to skip ahead to the #1 pick. The goal here is to discuss and analyze filmmaking, not to choose an order of best to worst. Now that we've got that out of the way, please sit back, relax, and take a journey with me fifteen years in the past, as we examine some of the best cinema has offered.

- Chris Stuckmann

2000-2003

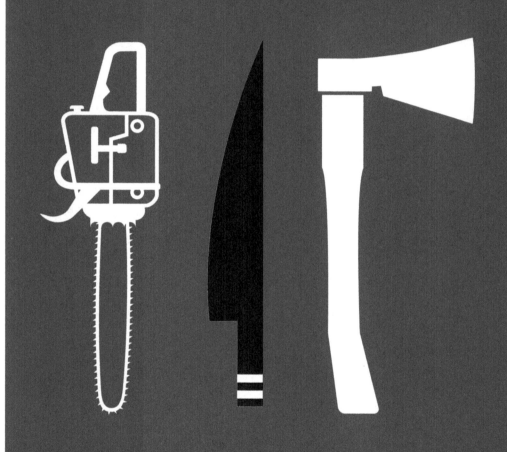

AMERICAN PSYCHO (2000)

DRAMA

Director:
Mary Harron

Starring:
Christian Bale
Jared Leto
Reese Witherspoon

Studio:
Edward R. Pressman
Productions

Serial killers. Hollywood seems obsessed with the sub-genre. Films like 1995's *Se7en* explore violent crimes through the eyes of the detectives attempting to solve them. *American Psycho* provides a refreshing change of pace by placing us in the expensive shoes of Patrick Bateman, a slick-haired, high-powered businessman played to sarcastic brilliance by Christian Bale. He's the type who arrogantly flies into a fit of envy at the sight of an associate's extravagant business card. "Look at that subtle off-white coloring, the tasteful thickness of it. Oh my God. It even has a watermark!"

His business card may be lacking, but Bateman seems to have it all. Riches, status, women. Unfortunately, despite his money and position in life, he can't seem to stop murdering people.

The power of *American Psycho* lies in the mystery surrounding Bateman's horrific acts of violence. Are his crimes real? Or is the whole ordeal some terrifying lucid dream existing only in his mind? The film traverses his mental anguish in a way I find most remarkable, and it does so with an impressively wicked sense of humor. Few films can get a laugh out of a bloodied, naked man chasing a woman with a chainsaw. Or how about Bateman's compulsion for quoting 80s pop music? "Do you like Phil Collins?"

American Psycho is shot with meticulous attention to detail. Nearly every frame contains something visually arresting. In fact, I think many people overlook the immaculate cinematography when remembering this film. But I can't really blame anyone for that, since the dialogue and performances are both so infectiously endearing. Factor in the biting satire of 80s culture along with two great supporting turns from Jared Leto and Reese Witherspoon and you really have no excuse to miss it. Unless of course, you have to return some videotapes.

MEMENTO (2000)

MYSTERY | THRILLER

Director:
Christopher Nolan

Starring:
Guy Pearce
Carrie-Anne Moss
Joe Pantolino

Studio:

Most films play out in a three-act structure. The format is an effective way to ratchet up tension, yet its familiarity causes us to anticipate events to the point where few films actually surprise us anymore. *Memento* flipped that upside down… or should I say, reversed it?

As someone who personally knows how difficult selling an original screenplay is, I can't imagine the conversations Christopher Nolan had as he pitched his chronologically reversed story, but somehow, it actually got made. *Memento* is a gigantic celebration of risk-taking, and man, did it ever pay off!

The always underrated Guy Pearce deftly inhabits the nerve-racked character of Leonard, a man hunting for his wife's murderer while using a complex system of tattoos and notes to help him remember important details. He has no short term memory you see, he forgets everything that just occurred to him within minutes.

The narrative runs backward, from end to beginning. That's right, you heard correctly. Someone made a backward-running film with a lead character who forgets what he's doing every few minutes, and somehow it's one of the best films ever made. Did I mention there are black and white scenes inter-spliced throughout, and that those are sequential? Wait, where was I?

Nolan's incredible understanding of storytelling—in reverse, no less—is endlessly inspiring. Amongst all the psychological thrills, the film somehow manages to be deeply touching. Leonard often pauses to reminisce on the intact memories of his wife, and these scenes are brimming with tragic melancholy. We know that, within minutes, he won't recall his brief second of happiness, and instead will look from side to side, wondering how he got there. *Memento* is a stunning achievement in original filmmaking, with an affecting story that has yet to be paralleled. I doubt it ever will.

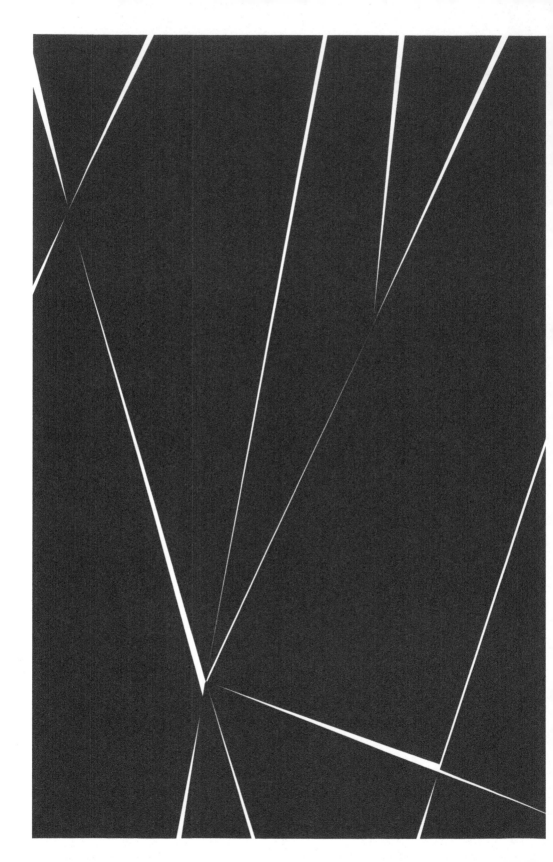

UNBREAKABLE (2000)

DRAMA | MYSTERY | SCI-FI | THRILLER

Director:

M. Night Shyamalan

Starring:

Bruce Willis

Samuel L. Jackson

Robin Wright

Studio:

Touchstone Pictures

When M. Night Shyamalan hit it big with *The Sixth Sense* (1999), many thought he could go nowhere but down. In fact, many think that's exactly what he did. When you write and direct a film that audiences, critics, and even the Academy love, I can't imagine how one might approach a follow up. These are just a few of the reasons I think *Unbreakable* is not only a superior film when compared (unjustly) to *The Sixth Sense*, but put simply, one of the best superhero movies ever made.

Unbreakable is so vastly different from other films in its genre. It was a particular departure for Shyamalan, who feared being put into what he calls "The Box." He wanted to do something original rather than get pigeonholed. "Original" can be a dirty word in Hollywood, a dangerous word. Yet Shyamalan pulled it off.

In *Unbreakable*, everyman David Dunn (Bruce Willis, in his best performance to date) survives a train wreck without a scratch. Comic book art gallery owner Elijah Prince (Samuel L. Jackson and his hair) tries to convince David that he's a superhero placed on Earth to protect the human race. David doesn't pay him much mind, but as the impossibilities mount—imperviousness to illness, heretofore-unknown strength—David begins to wonder.

What follows is one of the most unique and deeply moving films I've ever seen. Shyamalan took a major chance with *Unbreakable*, and while it was initially dismissed as an inferior film, one not worthy of the man who made *The Sixth Sense*, its reputation has grown over the years. Today, it's often lauded as being ahead of its time, predating the comic book movie boom. Even the great Quentin Tarantino referred to it as "one of the masterpieces of our time." The film is worth seeing for James Newton Howard's brilliant compositions alone, which are haunting, powerful, and even inspiring.

My advice? Don't compare *Unbreakable* to Shyamalan's other works. Appreciate it instead for what it is: a fascinating tale of a superhero in hiding.

CROUCHING TIGER, HIDDEN DRAGON (2000)

ACTION | DRAMA | ROMANCE

QUICK FACTS

Director:
Ang Lee

Starring:
Zhang Ziyi
Michelle Yeoh
Chow Yun-fat

Studio:
COLUMBIA PICTURES

As a youth, I had an unhealthy fascination with Bruce Lee's animalistic battle cries. He didn't just knock someone out, he let everyone in the building know he was coming. Growing up, his signature shrieks and howls were parodied so often, it seemed that martial arts films were losing their impact. Perhaps Jackie Chan observed this rift, leading to his successful inclusion of physical comedy amongst his epic butt-kicking. My enchantment with this filmmaking style continued with such films as The *Matrix*, but as time passed, it slowly became clear that the martial arts film was dead.

A thrilling resurgence occurred when *Crouching Tiger, Hidden Dragon* broke international records, became the highest grossing foreign film in U.S. history, and walked away with four Oscars. Films spoken entirely in Mandarin Chinese simply didn't gross over $100 million in America. Ever. Ang Lee's beautiful tale of masters, apprentices, martial arts and love had broken down cultural barriers, paving the way for gorgeous films like *Hero* and *House of Flying Daggers*.

Yuen Wo Ping—renowned for his breathless fighting choreography in films like *Drunken Master*—achieved heart-stopping results with actors Chow Yun-fat, Michelle Yeoh, and particularly the luminous Zhang Ziyi. Her role as a rebellious governor's daughter facing an arranged marriage garnered much acclaim, and her striking command of swordsmanship and hand-to-hand combat made an undeniable impression.

Amongst all the breathtaking action are two touching stories of love and the circumstances which make grasping it impossible. These stirring, tender hardships give *Crouching Tiger, Hidden Dragon* its soul. Despite being set in a fantastical version of the past, its appeal is universal. It remains one of the few martial arts films that successfully combined marvelous action with a poignant story.

SPIRITED AWAY (2001)

ANIMATION | ADVENTURE | FAMILY | FANTASY

QUICK FACTS

Director:

Hayao Miyazaki

Starring:

Mari Natsuki

Bunta Sugawara

Miyu Irino

Studio:

スタジオジブリ
STUDIO GHIBLI

Hayao Miyazaki has created more masterpieces than your average filmmaker has created films. The sheer force of his talent has been felt since *The Castle of Cagliostro*, and he's remained relevant as an artist, while also being a vastly inspirational individual. (Watch the documentary *The Kingdom of Dreams and Madness* and share my awe at his seemingly tireless work ethic.) He's won countless awards in his field and has been lauded as one of animation's greatest visionaries.

Why am I telling you all this? Because it's astounding to me that *Spirited Away*, perhaps his greatest work, is so fiercely humble in mentality, free of all disdain, cynicism, and pessimism that could stain its childlike beauty.

The story encompasses a naive girl who stumbles off the beaten path and finds herself at a bathhouse run by witches, spirits and godlike creatures. She must learn to work for a living while she's surrounded by entities that are vastly superior to her in strength and intellect, all while seeking a way to rescue her parents from the clutches of an evil spell.

Spirited Away is endlessly imaginative, filled with more wonder than any film of its kind. Studio Ghibli is renowned for its gorgeous and lifelike animation, but they truly outdid themselves. The scenic backgrounds are photorealistic, with lush valleys and plains blending into the horizon. Miyazaki also has a keen sense for sweeping, epic action, and *Spirited Away* is chockfull of jaw-dropping moments that send chills down my spine. I'm not exaggerating. There are many visuals in this film that genuinely make my hair stand on end.

If you've never seen a Studio Ghibli film, this would be a great place to start. It more than deserved its win for Best Animated Feature at the Oscars, and remains to this day the gold standard for animation around the world.

DONNIE DARKO (2001)

DRAMA | SCI-FI

QUICK FACTS

Director:
Richard Kelly

Starring:
Jake Gyllenhaal
Maggie Gyllenhaal
Jena Malone

Studio:

The term "cult classic" was invented specifically for films like Richard Kelly's *Donnie Darko*. Initially dismissed by the masses and denied by critics, its lasting appeal is indisputable and its cultural impact impossible to ignore. Put simply, *Donnie Darko* is too strange to forget.

On the surface, *Donnie Darko* is about young Donnie (Jake Gyllenhaal), who survives a near-fatal accident only to find himself haunted by visions of a large rabbit creature. That hook alone aroused my interest enough to seek the film out. Other canny filmgoers did the same, and they've been spouting hordes of theories, explanations, and analyses for years since.

Donnie Darko's wild originality can be a bit off-putting. I admit to leaving my first viewing disappointed. Yet as days passed, I found myself obsessing over the smallest details. A seed had been planted. What did that look mean? How does that make sense? Why was Donnie smiling? It's this power to stick in your thoughts that makes *Donnie Darko* stand out from the crowd.

The suggestion of time travel, mind-control, and the manipulation of the dead are ever present in the film's themes. Yet, somehow, Kelly deftly interweaves the deep exploration of such points with the early aughts high-school era. Donnie's introversion and odd ball tactics prove difficult for teachers, which leads to my favorite scene, in which Donnie questions the moral implications of a teacher's poorly conceived experiment. Watching Gyllenhaal in this scene is like seeing Michael Jordan in his prime. You just gave him the ball and let him rip.

Donnie Darko expertly mixes the crazy concoction of teen angst, spirituality, time travel and predestination, complete with a 6-foot rabbit. There really is no other film like it.

OCEAN'S ELEVEN (2001)

CRIME | THRILLER | COMEDY

Director:
Steven Soderbergh

Starring:
George Clooney
Brad Pitt
Matt Damon

Studio:
Jerry Weintraub
Productions

Remakes. Hollywood has a sickening obsession with them. "Remember that movie you loved as a child? Yeah, we were hoping to squeeze some more money out of it." Yet there can be gold in remaking a movie that had a great idea but failed to realize its full potential. Steven Soderbergh's *Ocean's Eleven* did just that, and it's one of the best remakes ever made.

Ocean's Eleven has the definition of an A-list cast. I mean, really, is this cast even fair? George Clooney, Brad Pitt, Matt Damon, Julia Roberts, and Andy Garcia, just to name a select few! Ted Griffin's witty script maximizes this plethora of talent: the interactions between and camaraderie among these thieves is one of the highlights of the film.

Soderbergh directs with brazen flair, and the film is sharply edited and gorgeously shot. That was no small feat. Having visited the MGM Grand, where a large portion of the movie was filmed, I can tell you it's not nearly as impressive in real life. Soderbergh did an amazing job glamming the place up. The breathtaking cinematography of *Ocean's Eleven* is criminally overlooked. The dreaded "mainstream fun" label kept the movie from getting the respect it deserved amongst cinephiles for years.

As a heist film, *Ocean's Eleven* is simply one of the best. Yet my favorite aspects have nothing to do with the heist. The real joy is watching these thieves crack wise. They're always winking at the audience in just the right ways.

MINORITY REPORT (2002)

ACTION | MYSTERY | SCI-FI | THRILLER

Director:

Steven Spielberg

Starring:

Tom Cruise

Colin Farrell

Samantha Morton

Studio:

We were driving to that childhood theater I mentioned in the introduction, Plaza Cinemas at Chapel Hill. Myself, two friends and their father. I was excited for the movie, but more so for the summer weather. Their Dad, however, began talking about Steven Spielberg's filmography, and suddenly, I found myself smack dab in the middle of my first real discussion about film. The year 2002 was instrumental in my life, providing me with many firsts. I have *Minority Report* to thank for introducing me to the idea of a healthy debate about movies.

The year is 2054. Tom Cruise plays John Anderton, a cop working for Precrime, an organization utilizing three twins with predictive abilities. These young siblings are capable of seeing murders before they occur, sometimes even days or weeks beforehand. It's Precrime's job to stop these murders from happening, but the real story kicks in when Anderton himself is implicated in a murder and goes on the run, attempting to prove his innocence.

Without a doubt, one of the most impressive aspects of *Minority Report* is its completely believable vision of a world where citizens sacrifice privacy for the comforts of security, technology, and consumerism. Your retinas are scanned everywhere you go, so purchase history can be tailored to you through advertisements. Spider-bots infiltrate your house to do police work in lieu of humans. Even the swipe technology shown in the film was suggested before the smart phone and tablet were available.

Thanks to an endlessly compelling protagonist, fine-tuned action sequences, and classic Spielberg humor, Roger Ebert called *Minority Report* the best movie of 2002. For me, it was my first theater experience that sparked a love for intellectual film debate.

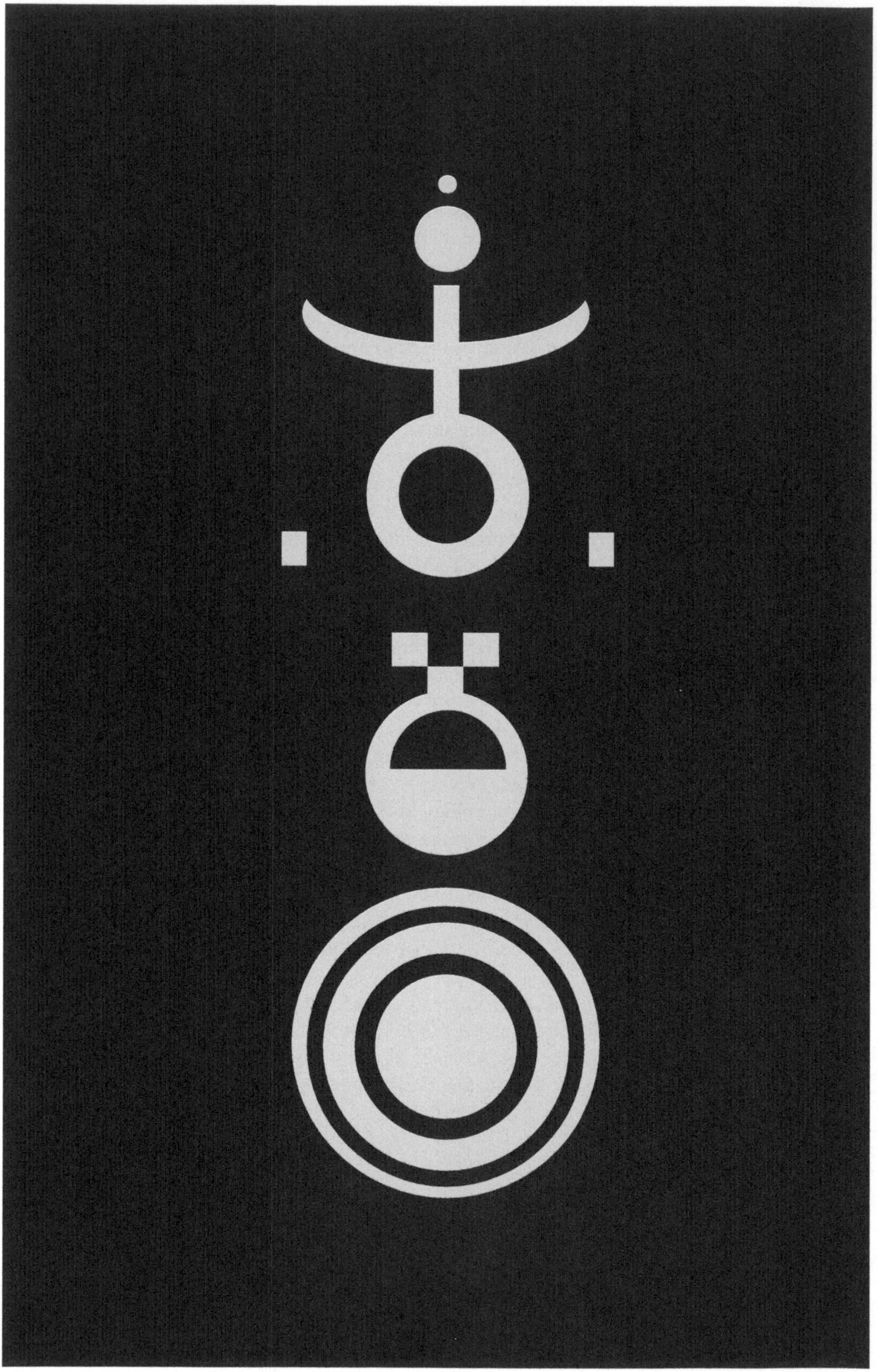

SIGNS (2002)

DRAMA | SCI-FI | THRILLER

Director:
M. Night Shyamalan

Starring:
Mel Gibson
Joaquin Phoenix
Rory Culkin

Studio:

 Touchstone Pictures

If you read the introduction to this book, then you already know how important this film is to me. It literally changed the way I view movies. The only reason I'm writing these words right now is because my mom took me to a theater in '02, changing my life. That night, I sat in my room, a new kid. *Signs* affected me so much that I even attempted to recreate the film in a shoddy and pointless shot-for-shot remake. Our resulting film was embarrassingly bad, but it undoubtedly communicated my love for filmmaking at that age.

Almost all the negativity I see directed at *Signs* are from complaints that universally miss the point. People tend to pile hate on Shyamalan because they watch his films from a very straightforward, wooden perspective. With most of his movies, and especially with *Signs*, this is not the right approach.

On paper, *Signs* is about a grieving family dealing with an alien invasion occurring around the world. Mel Gibson gives a harrowing performance as a former priest trying to protect his family from this otherworldly threat. Simply follow this plot, and *Signs* still works as a marvelously suspenseful, surprisingly funny thriller.

But where *Signs* truly shines is its brilliant subtext. The film is riddled with hidden meanings that few audiences pick up on. The loss of faith, denial of a higher power, Heaven, Hell, demons, angels, prophecies. Shyamalan's script and subtle art direction build a truly touching story, and one that many have overlooked.

You can watch *Signs* as enjoyable escapism and it still works. But if you're willing to dig a little deeper, I'm positive you'll discover a thematically rich and powerful work of art. It still hasn't stopped inspiring me, and it never will.

X2 (2003)

DRAMA | SCI-FI | THRILLER

Director:
Bryan Singer

Starring:
Patrick Stewart
Hugh Jackman
Ian McKellen

Studio:

2000's *X-Men* sparked a much-needed resurgence for comic book films. After a series of disappointing comics adaptations, Bryan Singer's work proved that spandex-clad men and women could carry a helluva kick-ass movie. And with *X2*, he did it again.

Hugh Jackman surprised everyone with his turn as Logan aka Wolverine, and with *X2* his character only deepened. The choice to center around the mystery of his past kept the series grounded, and also provided a compelling character arc, one that still continues today. Can you believe there was actually a time when people were angry that Hugh Jackman was cast as the hairy, cigar-smoking mutant?

While it's easy to view the *X-Men* films as fun popcorn flicks, if you dig a little deeper, you'll discover quite a bit of subtext and social commentary. The persecution of the mutants by "normal" people is the prevalent theme in the series, and *X2* showcased this more than its predecessor and even its sequels. The invasion of the school at night, in which armed guards take children as prisoners with no remorse was particularly effective.

X2 was considerably more well-rounded than the first, and still today competes with *Days of Future Past* when deciding which is best. The action is terrific, the characters are well translated from page to screen, and the conflict between mutants and humans speaks volumes. Like most great comic book films, the superhero costumes fade into the background, and the people wearing them drift to the forefront.

PIRATES OF THE CARIBBEAN: THE CURSE OF THE BLACK PEARL (2003)

ACTION | ADVENTURE | FANTASY

QUICK FACTS

Director:
Gore Verbinski

Starring:
Johnny Depp
Geoffrey Rush
Orlando Bloom

Studio:

If there was ever a film that required a watch simply for one character and one performance, it's *Pirates of the Caribbean: The Curse of the Black Pearl*, and it's because of Johnny Depp's Oscar-nominated turn as Captain Jack Sparrow.

When watching the "Making Of," the producers described a feeling of genuine worry during the first few weeks of filming. Cast and crew were unsure what to make of the half-drunk style Depp was going for. But apparently, upon seeing dailies, attitudes changed. Gratefully, Depp wasn't forced to alter his approach, and we were blessed with one of the most iconic film characters in history.

Gore Verbinski directed this tale, who to this day remains an underrated filmmaker. The CGI-heavy followups can make it easy to forget how well made Black Pearl really was. He deftly combines many classic elements of film into an exciting ride that rarely quits.

The following sequels diminished the impact of the character significantly, but the first film remains a true adventure, with classic swashbuckling action, dashing romance, and impressive visuals. It's not high art, but it's a damn good time, which is exactly what a film like this should be.

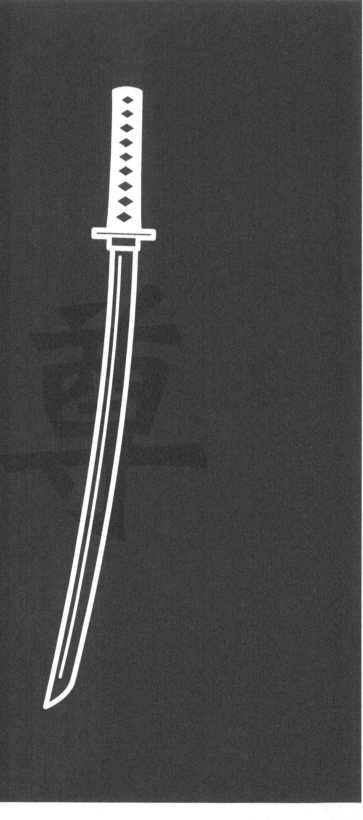

THE LAST SAMURAI (2003)

ACTION | DRAMA | HISTORY

Director:
Edward Zwick

Starring:
Tom Cruise
Timothy Spall
Ken Watanabe

Studio:
Radar Pictures

One of the most criminally overlooked films of the 00s is without a doubt *The Last Samurai*. Edward Zwick's gorgeous examination of the Samurai culture at the end of its reign flourishes into something new every time I watch it.

Tom Cruise plays Nathan Algren, an American solider in captivity, held by the Samurai. A friendship blossoms between him and Katsumoto (Ken Watanabe), a leader there, and soon he finds himself embracing the culture.

This is a gorgeous, stunning film that has more on its mind than eye-popping action scenes (which it also has in spades). Where the film really stands out is in the friendship between these two men, who could not come from more different backgrounds. It's an important tale about breaking barriers, honoring a culture, and discovering that your enemy just might not be your enemy.

OLD BOY (2003)

DRAMA | MYSTERY | THRILLER

Director:
Park Chan-wook

Starring:
Choi Min-sik
Yoo Ji-tae
Kang Hye-jung

Studio:

Show East
Egg Films

Have you ever heard about a film so often, that after a while, you almost feel obligated to watch it? It's almost as if you aren't actually a film lover until you see it. That's how I felt before watching *Oldboy*. For years, everyone from friends to viewers told me I had to see this film, and after seeing it, I understand why.

Oldboy is very original, not just in plotting, but in execution. A man is inexplicably locked in a room for 15 years, then released by his captor, only to become part of a deadly mind game. It's a suspenseful film with disturbing implications that change how you view the experience the second time around. It's that rare film that almost requires multiple viewings.

I won't dare spoil it for fear of ruining the impact, but I truly did not see the ending coming. It's a heartbreaking finale that causes one to shiver, feeling the horror and realization of our hero as he discovers the truth. *Oldboy* is directed with intensity, without holding back a single moment of dread.

Just do me a favor. Don't see the remake.

THE LORD OF THE RINGS: THE RETURN OF THE KING (2003)

ADVENTURE | DRAMA | FANTASY

QUICK FACTS

Director:
Peter Jackson

Starring:
Elijah Wood
Ian McKellen
Liv Tyler

Studio:

The word "epic"—overused as the term may be—was invented to describe movies like *Return of the King*. Every shot in Peter Jackson's magnificent finale to his beloved *Lord of the Rings* trilogy reflects a perfect bond between filmmaker and source material. Somehow, a movie over three hours long tears by, with your sore ass the only indication of time's passage.

Fellowship and *Towers* are both wondrous achievements, but *Return* captured the looming sense of dread and finality, at last providing closure to the journey of J.R.R. Tolkien's famous heroes and villains. *Return* harnessed a powerful emotional wallop, somehow making every scene feel grander than the last one.

In hindsight, it's amazing that the trilogy turned out as well as it did. Jackson filmed his opus back-to-back-to-back, which in the past has proven to be a terrible idea (*Matrix Reloaded* and *Revolutions*, anyone?). It's hard to correct one movie's mistakes when you're *already filming the next one*.

Yet, by some miracle, Jackson barely missed a step. *Return of the King* won 11 Oscars, an unprecedented feat for a "fantasy blockbuster"—two words that Academy members seem to loathe. To this day, it's one of the highest ranked on iMDB, and it's still visually spectacular 13 years after its release.

2004-2007

SPIDER-MAN 2 (2004)

ACTION | ADVENTURE | FANTASY

Director:
Sam Raimi

Starring:
Tobey Maguire
Kirsten Dunst
James Franco

Studio:

ENTERPRISES

The memory is still palpable. Summer of '04, waiting outside my neighborhood theater to get into the early showing of *Spider-Man 2*. Friends were meeting me soon! School was out! Spider-Man was here! Most critics and fans loved the first film, and Roger Ebert (who came away lukewarm on the original) had proclaimed this sequel the best superhero film he'd ever seen. The excitement for this film was legendary, and it didn't disappoint.

Sam Raimi's brilliant sequel took everything we loved about the first film, and brought the characters even more down to earth. Nerd-turned-superhero Peter Parker can't control his powers. Childhood flame Mary Jane Watson is marrying an astronaut, while best friend Harry Osborn boils with hatred for Spider-Man, blaming him for the death of his father. The screenplay piles sadness, pain, loss, and regret atop our hero, reflecting the greatest strength of the Peter Parker character: he's just like us.

Even more than its predecessor, *Spider-Man 2* understood that to relate to Spidey, we had to care about Peter. It also understood that great villains must be relatable, too, and *Spider-Man 2* features one of the greatest comic-book villains of all time: Doctor Otto Octavius (brought to life through Alfred Molina's darkly complex portrayal). Loss and tragedy inform Octavius's actions. He's not a vile man who bellows with laughter because he's just so darn evil. He's just a person. We empathize with him even as we condemn his deeds.

Since we see ourselves in the nerd behind the mask and the broken man behind four mechanical arms, watching these characters clash becomes enthralling. Of course, it helps that *Spider-Man 2* features one of the best action scenes ever made, a lightning-fast train sequence guaranteed to make your hair stand on end. The thrills combined with the heart make *Spider-Man 2* one of the greatest superhero films ever, and its eventual sequel and two reboots never came close to equaling it.

COLLATERAL (2004)

CRIME | DRAMA | THRILLER

QUICK FACTS

Director:
Michael Mann

Starring:
Tom Cruise
Jamie Foxx
Jada Pinkett Smith

Studio:

PARKES · MACDONALD
PRODUCTIONS

"Yo homie… that my briefcase?"

The first time I saw Michael Mann's *Collateral* was unfortunately not in a theater but rather my living room. I popped the DVD in well past midnight, completely ignorant that I was about to have a life-altering experience. By the end of the film, I had wrapped a blanket around myself, having pulled it up to my chin, mesmerized by the stunning vision of city nightlife and the crackling intensity of every single scene.

Tom Cruise plays Vincent, the coolest hitman alive. Vincent forces L.A. cabbie Max (Jamie Foxx, in an Oscar-nominated role) to drive him to his hits. The two form a strange, brotherly bond. Before the sun rises, both of them will have changed forever.

Collateral inspired me to notice the beauty of the city after nightfall: the ambience of orange and yellows, the subtlety of mist rising from sewer grates, the breeze passing between buildings. I even enlisted my friends to help me film a feature-length movie largely inspired by *Collateral.*

It was Mann's striking artistry combined with two unhinged performances that affected me so deeply. If *Signs* caused me to think differently about suspense, *Collateral* did that for action. Strangely though, it's a disservice to refer to *Collateral* simply as an "action movie" even though you may find the Blu-ray in that section. The film's true heft and impact come from the leads' journey and ultimate transformation. It's far more than just a series of action scenes. Indeed, the best action occurs when these two very different men find themselves verbally dueling within a claustrophobic cab.

During a panel at San Diego Comic Con, I was asked if I had a film I liked to show new friends, and without hesitation, I responded with *Collateral.* Its robust and thrilling action sequences, sizzling dialogue and Mann's signature romanticism of L.A. make it a surreal experience you won't soon forget.

THE INCREDIBLES (2004)

ANIMATION | ACTION | ADVENTURE

QUICK FACTS

Director:
Brad Bird

Starring:
Craig T. Nelson
Jason Lee
Holly Hunter

Studio:

The first time I saw *Toy Story*, I couldn't imagine anything topping it. In fact, it took nearly ten years for Pixar to make a film I viewed as an improvement. And here it is.

The Incredibles centers around a family of superheroes forced to lead normal lives when a lawsuit outlaws all superheroes. This is a brilliant idea. Imagine the Hulk sitting behind a desk at an insurance agency. Eventually, trouble inevitably brews and our heroes have to come out of retirement.

Brad Bird has become a household name, but with The Incredibles, he was still proving himself. Bird's *The Iron Giant* received critical praise upon its release in 1999, yet it was a financial bomb. *The Incredibles* helped put Bird on the map.

Like *The Iron Giant*, *The Incredibles* is a loving tribute to old-fashioned filmmaking. Heightened by a jazzy score from Michael Giacchino, the films vibrant visuals explode off the screen, no 3-D required. Even better than the animation, though, are the characters. They quite literally leap from the screen. The family dynamic is a huge part of the film's emotional heft, and it makes their eventual team-up all the more enthralling.

The Incredibles is tons of fun for everyone, but it's also an extremely smart film that still entertains today. Bird's energetic world is populated with superheroes that feel more human than the actual human stars of many lesser films.

SHAUN OF THE DEAD (2004)

COMEDY | HORROR

Director:
Edgar Wright

Starring:
Simon Pegg
Nick Frost
Kate Ashfield

Studio:

STUDIOCANAL

The first time I saw *Shaun of the Dead*, I had no idea what to expect. I don't believe I knew who Edgar Wright was, or what he'd done, because I saw this many years after its release. While watching, I remember thinking this was probably the first time I'd ever been genuinely riveted by a comedy.

Simon Pegg and Nick Frost floored me. I mean, they knocked me the hell out. Their comedic timing and "bromantic" chemistry was a thing of beauty. *Shaun of the Dead* came at just the right time for me. The comedy genre has suffered greatly from a lack of respect from studios and filmmakers over the years. The genre has been dominated by sophomoric humor and easy jokes for way too long, and *Shaun of the Dead* reminded me that there are people out there who actually care about making a good film.

It inspired the start of the "Cornetto Trilogy," consisting also of *Hot Fuzz* and *The World's End*, both terrific films in their own right. *Shaun of the Dead* might just be my favorite of them all, and not just because it was the first. It's freshly funny, surprisingly touching and at times, even a little scary. I hope Edgar Wright makes movies forever.

A HISTORY OF VIOLENCE (2005)

CRIME | DRAMA | THRILLER

QUICK
FACTS

Director:
David Cronenberg

Starring:
Viggo Mortensen
Maria Bello
William Hurt

Studio:

NEW LINE CINEMA

A History of Violence is a film I viewed with no preconceived knowledge of plot or story. At the time, I wasn't very well versed in David Cronenberg's filmography, and I had no idea what to expect. From the moment small-town restaurant owner Tom Stall (Viggo Mortensen) explodes in rage against the men robbing his establishment, I was consistently surprised with nearly every scene that followed.

The film also offers a chilling look at what the local news can do to someone who does something heroic. Your entire life can change, and that's not necessarily a positive thing. *A History of Violence* shows how a violent act can have dangerous repercussions on a family, a town, and one man's entire life.

The film is worth seeing not just because of its visceral direction and intense, frightening action, but also for a career-best turn from Viggo Mortensen, who generates great sympathy in the lead. His character holds many secrets, and so does the film. The journey we take as an audience to discover these secrets feels liberating and strangely life-affirming.

KISS KISS BANG BANG (2005)

COMEDY | CRIME | MYSTERY

QUICK FACTS

Director:
Shane Black

Starring:
Robert Downey, Jr.
Val Kilmer
Michelle Monaghan

Studio:

SILVER PICTURES

Kiss Kiss Bang Bang is a film I consider to be one of the most overlooked of the past 15 years. After the huge success of *Iron Man*, some have gone back to revisit Robert Downey, Jr.'s early works, and discovered this gem. For most however, it's never brought up.

The film follows a petty thief pretending to be an actor (Downey), and a private eye (Val Kilmer) trying to solve a murder. Shane Black (*Lethal Weapon*) wrote and directed this hilarious mashup of genres, and his crackling, witty dialogue and sharp eye for visual panache made *Kiss Kiss* a terrific time at the movies.

What makes the movie so unique is a combination of many different types of films, while still somehow maintaining a suspenseful, film noir vibe. It's also that rare film that feels completely in the moment, almost as if each scene wasn't planned, and somehow magically played out before our eyes. It's this euphoric feeling of inspiring spontaneity that makes every moment of *Kiss Kiss Bang Bang* pop with glorious fun.

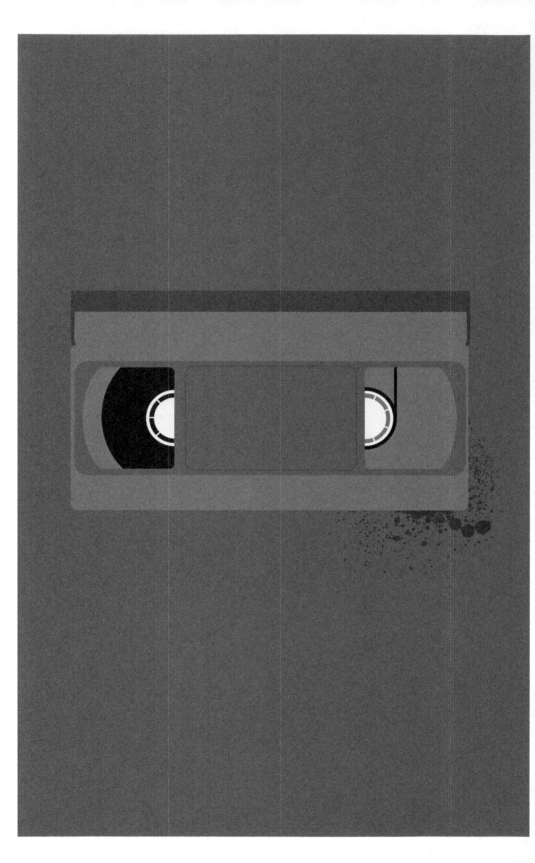

CACHÉ (HIDDEN) (2005)

DRAMA | MYSTERY | THRILLER

Director:
Michael Haneke

Starring:
Juliette Binoche
Daniel Auteuil
Maurice Bénichou

Studio:

Caché opens with a static shot of a quiet neighborhood, the kind of bold shot unseen in mainstream film that roots out impatient audience members. By my calculations, this shot lasts for just under three minutes, with very little movement occurring in frame. Before long, an uncomfortable sensation creeps through you, an unshakable paranoia that *something is wrong*. Movies aren't supposed to be like this. Why isn't anything happening? Should I be watching this?

Finally, the image changes. Tiny squiggly lines appear, indicating a rewinding tape. We realize a couple is watching the same thing we are on a videotape found at their door. It's a recording of their house, shot from an angle no camera could possibly reach. Honestly, can you think of something more terrifying than realizing your home is being watched? Who is the culprit? What does he want? Will he hurt my child?

Caché is less concerned with the answers to these questions, and instead remains focused on the turmoil they inflict on the lives of Georges and Anne Laurent, played exceptionally by Daniel Auteuil and Juliette Binoche. Arguments ensue as more tapes arrive at their doorstep, fracturing this troubled couple even further. Fastidious director Michael Haneke weaves a disturbingly realistic tale of divided culture, domestic disturbance, and the guilt of past sins. He shrewdly recognizes that despite the horror the videotapes suggest, the real terror is the skeletons in our closet.

Throughout the majority of the film, I found myself begging the screen for answers. I perused every frame meticulously, hoping to find any clue to the mystery. It's not until the final shot that Haneke finally gives us a drop of information. Within this frame, a disturbing suggestion is made, causing me to rethink the entire film. It's the type of conclusion that instantly makes you want to watch the movie again, but with a different perspective.

The audacious amount of respect Haneke is giving the audience is highly commendable. *Caché* requires patience, laser-focused observation, and a well-trained eye. If you have these, the mystery will become clear.

CASINO ROYALE (2006)

ACTION | ADVENTURE | THRILLER

QUICK FACTS

Director:
Martin Campbell

Starring:
**Daniel Craig
Eva Green
Mads Mikkelsen**

Studio:

EON
PRODUCTIONS

The reinvention of a popular franchise, a timeless classic, or in this case, a character, has spread through Hollywood like a disease. I'm thoroughly convinced that we'll receive at least one *Friday the 13th* incarnation every five years. (But hear me, studio executives: don't you dare touch *Jaws*. That's sacred ground.) The majority of these reboots and remakes aren't made with care, easily recognized as the blatant cash grabs they are. Gratefully, that wasn't the case with *Casino Royale*, Daniel Craig's first outing as the iconic spy, James Bond.

Casino Royale perfectly embodies—and more importantly, *understands*—the term "reboot." Less experienced filmmakers assume their reboot will be interesting simply because it contains beloved characters from previous films. But *Casino Royale* does for Bond what *Batman Begins* did for the Caped Crusader. Bond becomes a vulnerable human being, not just a gun-toting ladies man with a license to kill. He's vulnerable physically and emotionally. It's not the first attempt at humanizing Bond—he got married in *On Her Majesty's Secret Service*, after all. But it's the first time everything truly clicked.

Sean Connery's original achievement as the titular spy had few real competitors until Craig came along. His Bond is foolhardy, naive, and needlessly reckless, yet he's also fully committed to his job. In the past, Bond would allow his libido to jeopardize his assignments. In *Casino Royale*, Bond is getting frisky with a gorgeous lady yet leaves the instant she tells him what he needs to know. This is a cold, calculating assassin, and it's the closest we've gotten to Ian Fleming's original vision.

Simply from an action standpoint, this is the best 007 by far. Director Martin Campbell's mastery of set-pieces is evident with the visceral, jaw-dropping parkour sequence, legitimately one of the greatest action scenes ever created. The film also contains brilliant work from Eva Green, the best female character a Bond film has had in decades, and Mads Mikkelsen, the best Bond villain... ever. Mikkelsen's Le Chiffre is no cat-stroking caricature of evil. He's just a person, crippled by debt, scared of his enemies. I think that's why the film succeeds so well: it understands the characters inhabiting the screen, allowing their journey to propel the story instead of explosions and skimpy outfits.

THE DEPARTED (2006)

CRIME | DRAMA | THRILLER

QUICK FACTS

Director:

Martin Scorsese

Starring:

Leonardo DiCaprio

Matt Damon

Jack Nicholson

Studio:

WARNER BROS.

Martin Scorsese's journey to the Oscar was unimaginably long. Ever since flooring audiences with films like *Taxi Driver* and *Raging Bull*, that golden statue eluded him. Finally, in 2006, he struck Oscar gold with *The Departed*, an intense, hilarious and exhilaratingly sharp tale of cops and mobsters.

Leonardo DiCaprio is forced to go undercover to infiltrate a mob run by Jack Nicholson, and as he gets deeply involved, the people aware of his deception begin to dwindle in numbers. Will he successfully bring these criminals to justice, or end up with no one left on his side to prove his innocence?

There's so much to love in *The Departed*. From Scorsese's lightning-fast filmmaking, to the painfully biting dialogue, and my word, the performances! From Matt Damon's deceptive character to Alec Baldwin's cursing arguments with Mark Wahlberg. Let's not forget Nicholson, who just when you think has nothing new to offer, brings a powerhouse performance that feels almost effortless.

If you've never seen *The Departed*, it's essential Scorsese, and quite possibly my personal favorite of all his films. "Fahkin Fiyafightas."

THE BOURNE ULTIMATUM (2007)

ACTION | THRILLER

The Bourne Identity shocked many people. Matt Damon became a household name after his Oscar win for *Good Will Hunting*, but that name was tied solely to dramatic work. Few pictured him as mind-fractured assassin Jason Bourne, made famous by the Robert Ludlum novels. His performance and the fantastic film proved naysayers wrong, and the follow-up *The Bourne Supremacy* kept the adrenaline rushing. Yet as good as those films are, *The Bourne Ultimatum* is undoubtedly the best of the trilogy.

Bourne is an endlessly captivating character, largely due to his memory loss. After two films exploring his past, *Ultimatum* finally reveals the truth, providing some closure for our tortured hero. This wouldn't matter if director Paul Greengrass wasn't as interested in Bourne's pathos as he is his brawn. Every thrilling set-piece is bookended with tangible human drama. This striking combination of physicality and vulnerability make Bourne fascinating, and Damon plays him so well, it's impossible to imagine someone else doing it.

Ultimatum is often hailed as one of the best action films ever made, but why is that? The obvious answer is that the film never lets up. From scene one, you're on the ride. Bourne grappling with Desh, the thrilling rooftop chase, the race through Manhattan's streets: it's amazing stuff! But we're thrilled because, in between these big moments, Greengrass explores our hero's motivation, his pain, his anger. Because Bourne is such a compelling character, we're invested when he's jumping across balconies.

The Bourne Ultimatum is a fiercely enjoyable popcorn action film, but thanks to smart filmmaking, it reaches touching dramatic heights rarely seen in films of its kind. I couldn't be more excited for the next chapter.

ZODIAC (2007)

CRIME | DRAMA | MYSTERY

QUICK FACTS

Director:
David Fincher

Starring:
Jake Gyllenhaal
Mark Ruffalo
Robert Downey, Jr.

Studio:
Phoenix Pictures

Movies centered around true life events are often overblown dramatically, with details being added simply for thematic purposes. The words "based on a true story" are rarely taken seriously anymore, and why should they be? It's been proven time and again that artistic license has diluted and distorted facts just to jerk that extra tear out of our eyes.

This isn't to say that David Fincher's ingenious tale of the Zodiac killings didn't take some liberties. But it's unequivocally the most involving procedural drama since *All the President's Men*, and it leans on documented facts and information rather than shamelessly manipulative storytelling.

Like many of the films we've covered, *Zodiac* is so captivating because its characters actuate the story, rather than the plot dictating their behavior. Since we're so invested in these people, the robust runtime of 157 minutes never drags. Credit also the seamless editing, which blends decades together with such efficiency, it's a wonder the Academy overlooked it.

The film's energy rests on the shoulders of Jake Gyllenhaal, who portrays Robert Graysmith, a cartoonist working at the San Francisco Chronicle whose attempts to decode the famous *Zodiac* letters sink him into the deep abyss of obsession. His unhealthy fixation on the case is mocked by colleagues and law officials, with his family life suffering as a result of his absorption.

He finds momentary solace in reporter Paul Avery and Inspector David Toschi (performed to perfection by Robert Downey, Jr. and Mark Ruffalo), the only men who see merit in his findings. But as years pass, the case begins to eat away at the three of them, eroding their self-confidence, assaulting their backbone. Within time, they're a shadow of their former selves, beaten down by the lack of resolution, crushed by the weight of self-inflicted guilt.

Zodiac is fascinating, uncommonly suspenseful, completely engrossing, and highly underrated. As a true story, it's endlessly alluring, but it's even more compelling as a character study. Real reporters and inspectors often face this kind of anticlimactic irresolution. It haunts them, just as *Zodiac* will haunt you.

THERE WILL BE BLOOD (2007)

DRAMA

Director:
Paul Thomas Anderson

Starring:
Daniel Day-Lewis
Paul Dano
Ciarán Hinds

Studio:
Ghoulardi Film Company

Unlike any other film covered in this book, *There Will Be Blood* is worth watching on just the merits of its central performance alone. Daniel Day-Lewis' work as Daniel Plainview is considered by many as one of the greatest performances of all time. It's not just hype or Oscar bait. His work here is damn legendary.

The film tells the story of a prospector in the early days of the oil business, and his relationship with a young preacher in town (Paul Dano). What starts as a fairly straight-forward drama eventually turns painfully dark, its themes stretching far beyond what you might have expected.

It's these damp, grotesque psychological corners that director Paul Thomas Anderson explores so admirably. The growing distrust between these two men, the thrilling religious subtext, and the underlying horror of parent-hood gone wrong make *There Will Be Blood* a wonderfully unique film, and one I'll never forget.

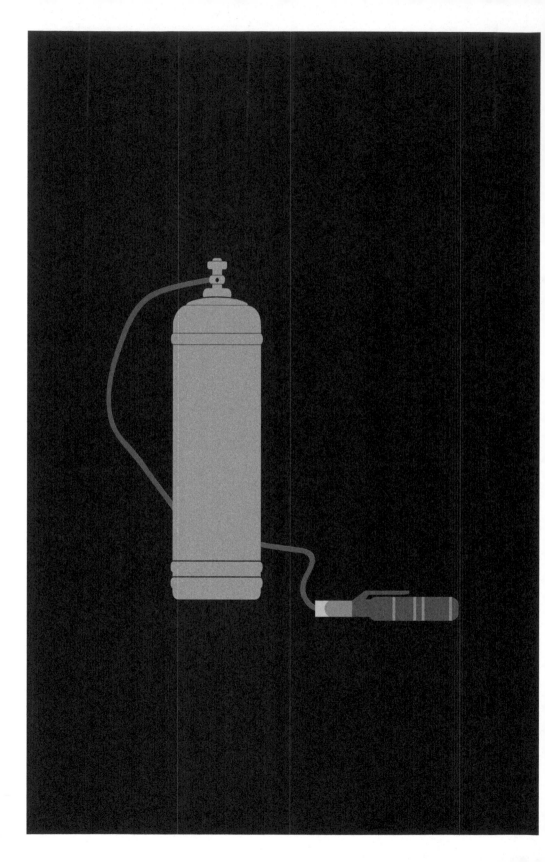

NO COUNTRY FOR OLD MEN (2007)

CRIME | DRAMA | THRILLER

QUICK FACTS

Director:

Joel and Ethan Coen

Starring:

Tommy Lee Jones

Javier Bardem

Josh Brolin

Studio:

The Coen brothers have always been universally talented. Their understanding of screwball comedy and tense drama has impressed me for years. You may think I've included *No Country For Old Men* in this book simply out of obligation, as if it's just one of the movies that had to be discussed. But on the contrary, I had a very love-hate relationship with this film at first.

I came close to hating *No Country* upon my first viewing. I'm sure the ending had something to do with that, but I also found the film painfully boring. But as weeks went on, I recall not being able to remove the film from my mind. To my surprise, I discovered a desire to watch it again, and I eventually did.

With that second viewing, and the subsequent watches in the future, I began to notice so much that I missed the first time, and I grew to deeply respect the filmmaking, and gorgeous cinematography. *No Country For Old Men* is one of those rare films that seems to grow and change every time you watch it. For that reason alone, it deserves to be in this book.

TRICK 'R TREAT (2007)

QUICK FACTS

Director:
Michael Dougherty

Starring:
**Anna Paquin
Brian Cox
Dylan Baker**

Studio:

For myself, a select few films are destined to maintain a connection with a certain time of year. Autumn simply hasn't arrived until John Carpenter's *Halloween* has knifed its way into my home, and the snow hasn't really fallen until *Home Alone* has jingled through my ears. A lesser known film than either of the aforementioned, the relentlessly fun *Trick 'r Treat* has nonetheless steadily gathered cult appeal, becoming a staple of my October each year.

Director Michael Dougherty smartly spins four stories, all occurring on Halloween night, into one big picture. The stories feature a cranky old man (Brian Cox) who hates the holiday and loathes trick-or-treaters, a young woman (Anna Paquin) who's mocked for her virginity, a group of children recalling a past tragedy, and a school principal (Dylan Baker) who seems to be hiding something in his backyard. Haunting them all is an odd little child wearing disheveled pajamas and a burlap sack over his head. He has an unusual affinity for lollipops and crawling on the ceiling.

Anthology films are notoriously problematic, largely because there's always one story in the bunch that doesn't grab you like the others. Often, you spend the majority of the film waiting for the inevitable connection to occur, uniting the storylines as one. *Trick 'r Treat*'s tales are uniformly excellent, however, and they boast ingenious connective tissue. If an unexplained event in one segment leaves you scratching your head, rest assured that a following story will provide the missing link. This supports the illusion of a creepy, lived-in neighborhood where actions have repercussions.

The list of films that successfully harness the joyous and gleeful abandon of Halloween while managing to frighten is very small. *Trick 'r Treat* wonderfully captures the warm, crisp feel of autumn, the charm of trick-or-treating, and yet somehow manages to be consistently unpredictable and terrifying. Track down the Blu-ray! You just might discover a new yearly tradition.

2008-2011

THE DARK KNIGHT (2008)

ACTION | CRIME | DRAMA

Director:
Christopher Nolan

Starring:
**Christian Bale
Heath Ledger
Aaron Eckhart**

Studio:

What's there to say about *The Dark Knight* that hasn't already been said? You know the ropes. Heath Ledger. The Joker. End of story. So rather than regurgitate the same praise you've heard countless times, I'll tell you a story.

The line stretched all the way through the parking lot, nearing the street. Even at night, the air was thick, sticky and hot. You could feel the anticipation in the air. My friends and I had advance tickets to the midnight show, and apparently a lot of other people had the same idea, because the theater had reserved something like ten auditoriums all night.

I remember a brief few minutes when a fear passed through our section of the line, a fear that we wouldn't get in, due to the insurmountable amount of people ahead of us. But to our joy, we proceeded into the theater, which may have been even hotter than outside. I recall many people wondering if they'd forgotten to turn the air conditioning on. We were packed into the room like little sardines in a small tin can, I don't think there was a single extra seat.

As the movie started, my mouth rarely stayed closed as the bank robbery scene played out. Heath's introduction and his line, "I believe whatever doesn't kill you simply makes you… stranger," didn't even receive applause. We were all in awe. But I will never, *ever*, forget what happened next. The pencil trick scene. You know what I'm talking about. When Joker slams the thug's head onto the table, my audience gasped, and remained in brief shock. A couple seconds went by, followed by a little quiet chuckling, and then the entire theater erupted with uproarious laughter. Nolan and Ledger had done it. We were in. The rest is history.

I remember sitting with my friends at four in the morning, all of us gathered in their living room, eating Taco Bell, talking about *The Dark Knight*. Seven years later, we're still talking about it.

CORALINE (2009)

ANIMATION | FANTASY

Director:
Henry Selick

Starring:
Dakota Fanning
Teri Hatcher
John Hodgman

Studio:
LAIKA

It's easy to watch a film, enjoy the experience, and remain completely oblivious to the effort put into it. If you're reading this book, I'm assuming you're one of those few who appreciate the hard work of gifted filmmakers. You pride yourself in learning about the hardships of filmmaking and examining the way a film is structured.

I share your passion, and that's why the stop-motion animation in *Coraline* impresses me so much. If you've ever attempted this style of filmmaking (as I have, poorly), you know that an hour of work hand-positioning characters might garner a brief second of actual footage. Yet *Coraline* is 100 minutes of creepy, surreal adventure without even a hint of tediousness.

My love for *Coraline* is due not only to the stellar animation but to the darkly moving story. It's both frightening and wonderful to watch young *Coraline* discover the magical world through the hole in the wall. Her awe turns to horror upon realizing that this world is a terrifying mirror image of her own, populated with doll-like versions of everyone she loves. That's disturbing, but the payoff is beautiful. It's the kind of movie that terrifies you as a child. Then you grow up and realize, "Wow, there was so much more to that freaky film that scared the bejesus out of me as a kid!"

Coraline is uncommonly mature in its exploration of family struggles, adolescence, and the desire to be loved. Thematically, it's shockingly rich, treading far more emotional ground than other films of its kind. If *Coraline* slipped under your radar, I highly recommend giving it a watch.

(500) DAYS OF SUMMER (2009)

COMEDY | DRAMA | ROMANCE

QUICK FACTS

Director:
Marc Webb

Starring:
Zooey Deschanel
Joseph Gordon-Levitt
Geoffrey Arend

Studio:

DUNE
ENTERTAINMENT

The words "romantic comedy" send shudders through me. Why are romantic comedies so high on my list of most loathed genres? In a word: predictability. Observe:

1. Two people meet.
2. A romantic spark occurs.
3. Montage of happiness.
4. They have an argument.
5. Montage of sadness.
6. They get back together.
7. Pop song plays over credits.

(500) Days of Summer plays with the tropes of the genre for a while, before pulling the rug out from underneath, sending you head-first into a wall. It's this defiant stance against cliché that makes the film special.

When Tom (Joseph Gordon-Levitt) meets Summer (Zooey Deschanel), he seems instantly infatuated by her luminous beauty, and everything else about her. As time goes by, problems surface, and the film takes a dramatic u-turn that captures the horror of unrequited love.

Having lived through a startlingly similar experience, I can tell you there's no other film that harnessed this particular brand of pain so aptly. I recall my catharsis as I drove home from the theater. It takes a person who's lived heartache to write this honestly, so I believe co-writer Scott Neustadter when he claims that 75% of the story really happened to him.

Today's rom-coms and pop songs lie to us. Love is hard. Really, really, *really* hard. There's no such thing as perfection. *(500) Days of Summer* is one of the most honest portrayals of this painful truth.

INGLOURIOUS BASTERDS (2009)

ADVENTURE | DRAMA | WAR

QUICK FACTS

Director:
Quentin Tarantino

Starring:
**Brad Pitt
Diane Kruger
Christoph Waltz**

Studio:

A BAND APART

Inglourious Basterds opens on a small farm. A burly man is chopping wood. His family is inside. In the distance, vehicles approach. The burly man's eyes fill with dread upon seeing the convoy. Enter Col. Hans Landa, "The Jew Hunter." His appearance on this farm signaled the arrival of Christoph Waltz, in an Oscar-winning role. The scene that follows is so white-knuckled, it may just be the most suspenseful Tarantino has ever generated.

That suspense is maintained throughout the entirety of *Inglourious Basterds*, a film that follows the separate storylines of multiple characters trying to survive Nazi-occupied France. Tarantino's typically magnetic dialogue beautifully realizes these diverse characters. With stunning cinematography and production design, *Inglorious Basterds* might just be his most gorgeous film yet.

Brad Pitt's turn as Lt. Aldo Raine is pure comic gold—his gravelly, exaggerated voice just begs impersonation. Speaking of comedy, Tarantino was surprisingly adept at setting up jokes that wouldn't receive payoff for quite some time. For instance, Aldo mentions early on that he and his men can speak Italian, but it's not until much later that the joke comes to fruition. "Bonjourno!"

The film also introduced me to the talent of Michael Fassbender, centerpiece of the electrifying bar shootout scene. My father was born in Germany and I spent the better part of my youth listening to German-speaking grandparents. Fassbender's perfect accent and inflection was music to my ears.

Choosing a favorite Tarantino film is daunting. His filmography isn't as vast as others, yet nearly every film he's made is next to flawless. Despite this, Inglorious Basterds is still my most beloved of his works. The suspense, comedy, and particularly the craft are all constantly on point. It's a history-bending laugh riot from start to finish.

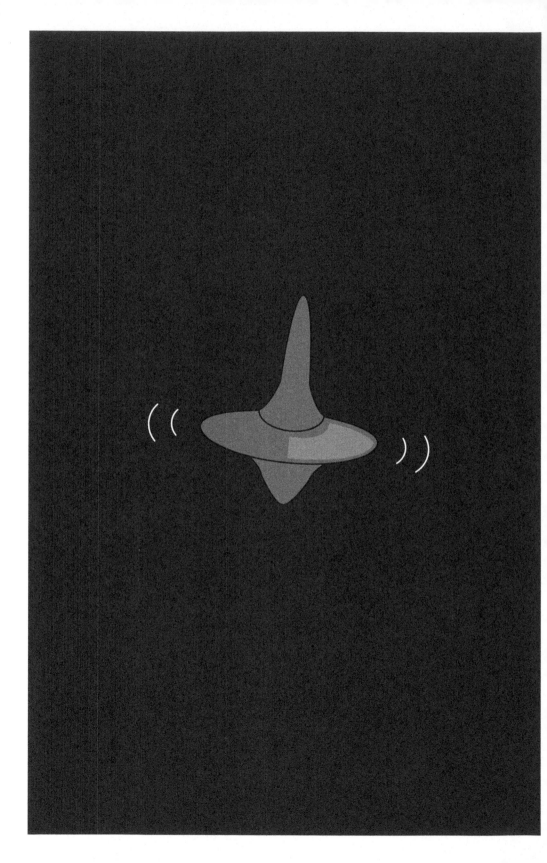

INCEPTION (2010)

ACTION | MYSTERY | SCI-FI

Director:
Christopher Nolan

Starring:
Leonardo DiCaprio
Joseph Gordon-Levitt
Ellen Page

Studio:

LEGENDARY

It's been a privilege watching Christopher Nolan rise from clever indie filmmaker to world renowned master. I've already discussed *Memento's* impact on me, and I still remember taking the DVD to friends and family, trying to force that genius upon them. When *Batman Begins* was coming out, my friends had no confidence in the film despite my argument that Nolan would do the character right. We know the outcome of that story.

Five years later, nobody was doubting Nolan anymore. Yet Nolan's successes were so known that many felt he'd plateaued. There's an inherent pessimism amongst film lovers about whether a filmmaker can continue to impress them. And Nolan still wowed audiences once again with his jaw-dropping, mind-bending, time-altering science fiction powerhouse *Inception*.

Inception revolves around dreams: namely, the infiltration of them. Nolan wisely utilized the virtually limitless scenarios a dream world might conjure, placing his characters in a positively unpredictable environment, one that feels so real despite being anything but. Think of all those times you've woken in the middle of the night certain you're falling, certain you're suffering pain. Yet it's just your brain sending false sensations. Nolan harnessed these sensations and created an entire universe around them.

Leonardo DiCaprio plays a father fleeing from a dark past and a dead wife who's there one moment and gone the next. Want to have a little fun? Look for his wedding ring appearing and disappearing throughout the movie. This isn't a continuity error: it's just another example of the small details that add deep layers to Nolan's films.

With each passing second, *Inception* threatens to descend into lunacy. There are so many rules to Nolan's world that have to be explained, sometimes through tons of exposition. But through dedicated performances, gravity-defying action sequences, and Nolan's *unbreakable* commitment to his story, *Inception* entertained unlike any film released in 2010.

TOY STORY 3 (2010)

ANIMATION | ADVENTURE | COMEDY

Director:
Lee Unkrich

Starring:
Tom Hanks
Tim Allen
Joan Cusack

Studio:

Something that stood out to me as I sat in the theater before *Toy Story 3* began, was just how many adults were present. Adults with no children with them, grown men and women who grew up in the 90s with the original Pixar classic.

The *Toy Story* series has always spoken to all ages. It's universally loved across generations because its themes stretch beyond childhood. *Toy Story 3* was smart to realize that childhood ends, and it didn't shy away from that bittersweet and tragic feeling. Woody and Buzz watch in horror as their beloved Andy grows up, and the story that follows is touching, tear-jerking and even poignant.

At the same time, the brilliant sense of humor that its predecessors had is ever prevalent. *Toy Story 3* is a very funny movie, and one that understands its place in the canon of animation history. It never attempts to cash in on nostalgia, but always remains fresh and relevant. It's one of Pixar's best!

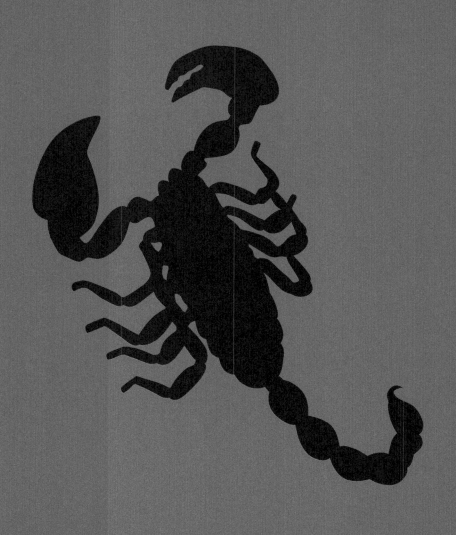

DRIVE (2011)

CRIME | DRAMA

QUICK FACTS

Director:
Nicolas Winding Refn

Starring:
Ryan Gosling
Carey Mulligan
Bryan Cranston

Studio:

Ryan Gosling plays a nameless criminal who offers nightly services as a getaway driver, while working as a stunt driver for movies by day. Similar to many films of this nature, his dark ways are upset by the new presence of a woman (Carey Mulligan) and child who happen to be his neighbors. His quiet life changes for the worse when he agrees to a job that might help them. With this choice, the suspenseful drama turns into a blood-soaked tragedy, dripping with tension and atmosphere, evoking classic film noir.

I've had many experiences leaving a theater surprised by the quality of the film, having gone in with a certain expectation. I suppose that's not a very wise mentality, but it's difficult to turn that part of your brain off when you're so inundated with an endless string of mediocre entertainment. I recall seeing *Drive* at a packed screening of action hungry viewers, people who had likely watched the fast-paced trailer, ecstatically ready to see the Ryan Gosling version of *The Transporter*. As you may know, the majority were immeasurably disappointed. I remember being the sole supporter of the film amongst my friends.

One of my fondest memories that day was walking out of the theater, looking up at the stars, and truly feeling rejuvenated. *Drive* didn't just surprise me, it utterly floored me. I had never seen a film like it, not ever. Nicolas Winding Refn's gorgeous vision of nightlife in L.A., the sizzling opening scene, the electronic, trancelike soundtrack, and the shocking outbursts of violence had scorched my brain. I never looked at film the same way again.

Drive is a film that improves infinitely with each viewing. Nearly every time I pop in the Blu-ray, something new materializes that had gone unnoticed before. It's this transformative quality that makes it such a rich and special movie, and the continual division of its audience that make it ripe for heated debates amongst film nerds, myself included. So grab a chair, let's talk about *Drive*. I could go for hours.

MISSION IMPOSSIBLE: GHOST PROTOCOL (2011)

ACTION | ADVENTURE | THRILLER

QUICK FACTS

Director:
Brad Bird

Starring:
Tom Cruise
Jeremy Renner
Simon Pegg

Studio:

BAD ROBOT

The Mission: Impossible series has proven not only resilient but dynamic (save the second film, which I believe featured more slow motion than all three *Matrix* films combined). The first film—steeped in government espionage, intrigue, and suspense—helped catapult Tom Cruise into action movie stardom. The third film was definitely a step in the right direction after the disappointing second installment, yet it surprisingly remains the lowest-grossing film in the franchise. Then came *Ghost Protocol*, and everything changed.

Cruise has stated his preference for a different director helming each installment, an approach that has kept the series fresh. *Ghost Protocol* was directed by Brad Bird, who before this film was known primarily for his excellent animated features *The Iron Giant*, *The Incredibles*, and *Ratatouille*. He brought laser-edged sleekness to the action sequences, the highlight being the nerve-racking Burj Khalifa scene in which Cruise—performing his own stunts—crawls along the side of the world's tallest building.

M:i:III brought the franchise back from the ashes, but *Ghost Protocol* reinvigorated it with a seamless blend of humor, suspense, action, and character. It also understood the importance of the team dynamic, wisely putting our heroes and their technology in constant disarray. In many ways, it's the perfect spy film: it never extends its reach beyond its grasp.

I feel fortunate to have seen the film in IMAX during its early run, since all Blu-ray transfers restrict the film to the common 2.35:1 aspect ratio. In the IMAX print, the black bars lining the top and bottom of the screen disappeared during some scenes, extending our view of the big moments. Those action scenes thoroughly engulfed me. Hopefully, there will someday be a release that honors this aspect ratio.

2012-2015

THE AVENGERS (2012)

ACTION | SCI-FI | THRILLER

QUICK FACTS

Director:
Joss Whedon

Starring:
Robert Downey, Jr.
Chris Evans
Scarlett Johansson

Studio:

ENTERPRISES

Growing up, *The Avengers* was a film no one thought would happen. Iron Man, Captain America, Hulk and Thor in the same movie? Impossible! Tons of barriers existed, too, including ironclad rights issues with multiple studios—issues that still exist today. (Spider-Man and Wolverine anyone?)

How could a writer take so many larger-than-life characters and create a balance that actually worked? Marvel's answer to that question was the Marvel Cinematic Universe, a film series that tied multiple storylines together, connecting gaps in story canon that individual films could never bridge in isolation. Rather than introducing each superhero in one film, Marvel could take their time with these characters, giving them each the separate attention they deserved. The MCU launched with 2008's highly successful *Iron Man*, which ended with a cheer-inducing after-credits scene. *The Avengers* lived up to that scene's promise despite sky-high expectations.

King of nerds Joss Whedon was chosen to write and direct. He brought his signature wit and a keen eye for action. More importantly, his clear understanding of these characters gave *The Avengers* a human touch, something lacking in most summer blockbusters. This is best illustrated by the team's failure to get along. Their arguments are entertaining but also speak volumes about their insecurities. Whedon's script wisely utilizes every opportunity to flesh out these characters, expanding the world even more.

Attempting to read between the lines with *The Avengers* is a pointless endeavor, and that's the way it should be. Hollywood's unnecessary desire to make every superhero film bleak isn't always the right approach. This film is a celebration of every kid's dream: seeing their heroes duking it out together. Comic lovers have been envisioning this since the 1960s, and it finally happened. Thank goodness it actually kicked ass.

SNOWPIERCER (2013)

ACTION | DRAMA | SCI-FI

Director:
Joon Ho Bong

Starring:
Chris Evans
Jamie Bell
Tilda Swinton

Studio:

THE WEINSTEIN COMPANY

Snowpiercer was a film released in American theaters, but I felt like I was in a different world while watching it. I knew I was seeing a film released by an American studio, but it truly felt like a foreign film.

Our story here is of a train, a corrupt justice system, and two classes of people: Poor and rich. The entire world has ended, and what remains is a snowy wasteland, and one train containing the rest of the population. At the back lie the passengers that are preyed on by the rich, high class citizens of the front cars. It's their thrilling revolt, led by Chris Evans— in his best performance to date— that made *Snowpiercer* so exciting.

The action sequences are tense and violent, accompanied by an almost dreamlike quality that sticks with you long after the film ends. I don't wish to spoil much, so I'll just leave it there. If you admire unconventional filmmaking, and action that feels new and different, check out *Snowpiercer*.

PRISONERS (2013)

CRIME | DRAMA | MYSTERY

QUICK FACTS

Director:
Denis Villeneuve

Starring:
Hugh Jackman
Jake Gyllenhaal
Terrence Howard

Studio:

ALCON
ENTERTAINMENT®

There was a time when movies deemed "thrillers" seemed more concerned with building suspense, crafting compelling characters, and taking time to tell the story. Movies like Francis Ford Coppola's *The Conversation* or Jonathan Demme's *The Silence of the Lambs* are a dying breed. Filmmakers of the past were more willing to spend the time examining their story deeply, exploring the dark corners of their characters and allowing them to blossom.

Today, the term "thriller" has been replaced with "action-thriller." Everyone's always sprinting somewhere or in the middle of an exchange that will soon lead them to a chase scene. Modern-day thrillers have lost a great deal of appeal by turning their focus from character to action.

This is why Denis Villeneuve's *Prisoners* left such an enormous impact on me. There's an intrinsic stillness to the film, a perverse desire to examine in detail the blackness of its story. No stone is left unturned, no grimy alley overlooked. A story about child abduction is bound to contain a sense of hopelessness, and *Prisoners* is steeped in it. Dread permeates every masterfully shot frame.

We observe Keller (Hugh Jackman), father and husband, combing the woods, calling out his daughter's name, all in vain. Most films centered around a missing person, especially a child, contain a ray of hope. In this bleak, cheerless film, one wonders if a happy ending is even possible. Detective Loki (Jake Gyllenhaal) knocks on doors and interrogates suspects, but immeasurable doubt infects every conversation. Villeneuve never gives us a second to breathe easy, not even a tiny chuckle. I've never seen a film that captures the crushing pain of uncertainty better than *Prisoners*.

The film's true interest, however, is moral ambiguity, the gray area between right and wrong. When Keller asks Franklin (Terrence Howard)—whose own daughter was abducted along with Keller's—to hold a possible suspect while he's beaten, it's the look of horror that crosses Franklin's face that Villeneuve wants to study. His uncommon restraint allows for a deep investigation of the dreary recesses of his character's minds that left me breathless a full minute after the film's end.

CAPTAIN AMERICA: THE WINTER SOLDIER (2014)

ACTION | ADVENTURE | SCI-FI

Director:
Anthony and Joe Russo

Starring:
Chris Evans
Samuel L. Jackson
Scarlett Johansson

Studio:

Growing up, the idea of seeing my comic book heroes on the big screen seemed like a dream. Thanks to the success of films like *Iron Man* and *The Avengers*, that dream is a reality. As much as I loved the aforementioned films, though, it was *Captain America: The Winter Solider* that brought harsh, unforgiving realism to the Marvel Cinematic Universe.

In 2012's *The Avengers*, Chris Evans played the powerful super-solider from the comics, shattering walls, doorways, and bones galore. Evans's portrayal—and the excellent script—made Captain America the most interesting Avenger on the team. *Winter Solider* understood that Cap's intense loyalty and unwillingness to betray his team—traits most said made him a boring character—were the qualities that made *The Avengers* the best Marvel film to that point. It turned these "perfect American" traits against Cap, forcing him to watch his once lauded stripes dragged through the mud.

The filmmakers famously approached the material as if they were helming a 1970's spy thriller rather than a big-budget superhero extravaganza. This unique angle elevated the material beyond a series of exciting set pieces. It added a layer of political and social depth unseen in previous MCU films.

If one were to judge Marvel's films solely based on their action sequences, *Winter Soldier* is their best by far. The highway assault sequence is viscerally thrilling. Notice the real fear on our heroes faces as they engage the bad guys. Never once do we feel these people are invincible, capable of surviving anything. That's a heck of a trick for a superhero film.

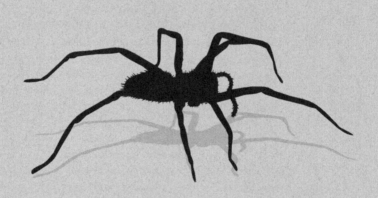

ENEMY (2013)

MYSTERY | THRILLER

Director:
Denis Villeneuve

Starring:
Jake Gyllenhaal
Mélanie Laurent
Sarah Gadon

Studio:
mecanismofilms

That spider… that freaking spider!

For a cinephile, there's nothing better than a confusing movie that begs them to hang around underneath the theater marquee, grasping at straws to decipher what they just saw. *Enemy* is directed by the immensely gifted Denis Villeneuve, starring Jake Gyllenhaal in a daringly restrained performance. So confounding is *Enemy* that as of this writing, over 770,000 baffled people have watched my analysis video in which I attempt to explain its hidden meanings. After initially seeing Enemy, I sat in awe at the puzzle pieces the film left scattered across the floor. It was almost as if Villeneuve was taunting me to approach this puzzle, and doing so took two months. Two months! Even now, as I write this, I'm positive there are still things I've missed.

I feel that with a film like this, you'd benefit to know little about the plot, so I won't say much besides the basics: Gyllenhaal is convinced he has an identical twin he never knew about, and is desperate to meet him. To assume this brief synopsis is all *Enemy* has to offer would be tantamount to observing one brick on The Great Wall of China and deciding you'd seen enough. This movie can actually be researched. Honestly ask yourself, when's the last time you saw a NEW film that actually required serious thought?

Enemy is part of a dying breed of films, and Villeneuve is clearly content with this. He actually had his cast sign an agreement to avoid discussing the meaning of the spiders that are ever present throughout the film. His intense dedication to his projects, especially *Enemy*, is remarkably refreshing in today's day and age of movies. Here's a movie that begs its audience to lean closer, wondering what exactly they just saw. A film that utilizes every space of the frame to populate the screen with clues and information. If that sounds intriguing to you then seek out this under-rated gem, just be prepared to take notes. Then watch it again, and take more notes. Then maybe lay in the fetal position, taking more notes.

UNDER THE SKIN (2014)

DRAMA | SCI-FI | THRILLER

QUICK FACTS

Director:
Jonathan Glazer

Starring:
Scarlett Johansson
Jeremy McWilliams
Lynsey Taylor
Mackay

Studio:
British Film
Institute

This is a weird one. A *very* weird one. So odd, in fact, that countless people denounced this film as one of the worst they've ever seen, while others hailed it as a spiritual successor to *2001: A Space Odyssey*. I can't know which side you'll fall on, but I can say with certainty that *Under the Skin* is a significant film and very much worth your time to track down.

To avoid unnecessary spoilers, I'll just say that *Under the Skin* is the story of a woman who prowls Scotland's city streets, preying on men drawn by her beauty. She invites these clueless men into her van and drives them to a black room, where something happens to them. Something terrible.

Scarlett Johansson was the perfect choice to play this feminine predator. It's the type of role one can't imagine another actor filling after watching her work. Her blank, emotionless expression as she ends lives is simply chilling.

This unnamed woman's journey is rarely expressed through dialogue, but rather through psychedelic imagery, through silent looks and reactions. Intrigue grows as she begins to transform, to awaken into a new self-awareness. Where this leads her is both fascinating and terrifying. The film's final five minutes still haunt me to this day.

If not for Jonathan Glazer's unique and beautiful vision—along with a horrifying score by Mica Levi—*Under the Skin* would've perhaps been a fun little movie. But with its unorthodox storytelling and its demand that you pay attention to every frame, the film is like a dark cave littered with provocative discoveries waiting to be unearthed. Respect the journey and you just might like what you find.

EDGE OF TOMORROW (2014)

ACTION | ADVENTURE | SCI-FI

Director:

Doug Liman

Starring:

Tom Cruise
Emily Blunt
Bill Paxton

Studio:

Despite strong reviews from press and public, *Edge of Tomorrow* opened at #3 at the box office, trumped by Disney's *Maleficent* and the book adaptation *The Fault in Our Stars*. Gratefully, the film's legacy didn't end with that disappointing opening, because it truly deserves the cult status it's earned among science fiction lovers.

Cruise stars as Cage, a reluctant military officer sent to the front lines of humanity's life-or-death battle against alien invaders. Cage's cowardliness was a mammoth surprise to filmgoers used to seeing Cruise portray heroic, fearless characters. But that's not the half of it: Cage falls on the battlefield. That's right: Tom Cruise dies! This shocking twist leads to an extremely funny character arc where Cage must adapt to the horror of reliving the same day over and over. The filmmakers wisely chose to find the dark comedy in this dark premise. Cage rebuilds himself from the ground up, becoming a better fighter and, ultimately, a better man.

Like Cage, *Edge of Tomorrow* gets better as it goes along. A high point is the introduction of Emily Blunt's character, Rita (though more popularly known as "The Full Metal Bitch"). Rita's reputation proceeds her, and she just might be the only person alive who can help Cage.

The film pays loving tribute to the brotherly camaraderie between soldiers, as portrayed in films like *Aliens* (Bill Paxton is even there!). Respect blossoms among Cage's teammates as Cage, through trial and error born of a thousand deaths, transforms from coward to alien ass-kicker. Watching his metamorphosis through their eyes is simultaneously hilarious and inspiring.

Edge of Tomorrow is a brilliant mashup of technically efficient camerawork, exciting stunts, and surprisingly hilarious dialogue and storytelling. If you missed it in theaters, seek out the Blu-ray. You won't regret it.

THE BABADOOK (2014)

DRAMA | HORROR | THRILLER

Director:
Jennifer Kent

Starring:
Essie Davis
Noah Wiseman
Daniel Henshall

Studio:

CAUSEWAY FILMS

The Babadook came out directly after two of the worst horror films of 2014: *Annabelle* and *Ouija*. It was the mixed concoction of seeing these films in short succession that inspired my video "The Problem with Horror Movies Today." In that video, I spoke about my exasperation with over-reliance on jump scares, CGI, and common horror tropes to make quick-and-dirty low-budget, high-profit horror. So thank you, *The Babadook*, for coming to my rescue.

Written and directed by first-timer Jennifer Kent, the film tells the tale of a single mother (Essie Davis) struggling to raise an unruly son who's convinced there's a monster living in their house. That's the easiest way to describe the film, but also the most trivial. The magic of *The Babadook* is what's lurking under the surface. Like all great horror, the real impact has nothing to do with the creature. It's the looming terror of mental illness, depression, grief, and the psychological torment of the widowed mother that's most horrifying. Her child won't stay out of trouble. Her friends give her judgmental looks. The neighbor is too nosy. And there's that unexplained black ash on her hands …

I usually don't make comments like this, but I truly think Essie Davis gives one of the best performances I've seen, especially when compared to other horror films. There's not one moment that her portrayal of this tortured woman doesn't convince. Watching her work sent chills through me in a way no jump scare ever could.

What's more frightening? A hand on the shoulder accompanied by a blast of unnecessary music? Or a woman struggling to raise her poorly behaved child while facing the twin monsters Depression and Loneliness? The first description is what most horror films today think is scary. *The Babadook* makes them look like G-rated kiddy fare.

BIRDMAN (2014)

COMEDY | DRAMA

Director:

Alejandro G. Iñárritu

Starring:

Michael Keaton

Zach Galifianakis

Edward Norton

Studio:

REGENCY®

Before *Birdman* took home the Oscar for Best Picture, I named it my favorite movie of 2014. I hadn't seen a single film that year that felt so alive. Every scene brimmed with energy and discovery.

From a filmmaking perspective, *Birdman* was jaw-dropping to behold. The entire film was shot and edited to appear as if it was one sustained take. There are times when a smart eye can tell a cut has been made, but really, what would be the point in looking for those moments?

Michael Keaton did his best work to date portraying a struggling playwright, desperately trying to put on an amazing show. But the film was really about his buried alter-ego, Birdman, a superhero he was well known for playing in the past. It was a very fun mirror image of the real life Keaton, so well-known for 1989's *Batman*.

The technique floored me, as did the performances. *Birdman* was not only a marvelously entertaining film, but one that had something very important to say about film criticism as an art.

WHIPLASH (2014)

DRAMA | MUSIC

QUICK
FACTS

Director:
Damien Chazelle

Starring:
Miles Teller
J.K. Simmons
Melissa Benoist

Studio:

There's a formula to "student-teacher" movies. We anticipate the beats almost unconsciously at this point: A hard working kid with a passion never gets noticed, until that fateful day when a good-hearted teacher takes note of his talent. *Whiplash* is less concerned with what we want to hear from teachers, and more concerned with telling us what we need to hear.

We suck. That's right. Whatever we think we're good at, we suck. At least, that's what Fletcher would tell us the second we stepped foot in his office.

J.K. Simmons won an Oscar for portraying the most foul-mouthed music instructor ever. He psychologically pummels his band into the ground, insulting them every chance he gets. The biggest target of his assault is the newbie, Andrew, a passionate drummer played by Miles Teller. The mind games that these two play with one another made *Whiplash* more than just a film about music. It's a borderline psychological thriller, and one of the best I've ever seen.

Editing alone makes this film worth watching. Moments are cut together almost like action scenes, with rapid-fire drumsticks pounding so fast that blood and sweat literally explode from the kit. This manic energy is reflected in Teller's fantastic work. He captures Andrew's bottomless passion beautifully.

Whiplash contains one of the greatest final scenes ever put to film, that actually made me want to cheer, for real. You've seen that quote before I'm sure, but with *Whiplash*, it's true.

WHEN MARNIE WAS THERE (2015)

ANIMATION | DRAMA | FAMILY

Director:
Hiromasa Yonebayashi

Starring:
Sara Takatsuki
Kasumi Arimura
Nanako Matsushima

Studio:

スタジオジブリ
STUDIO GHIBLI

Studio Ghibli is responsible for an unending list of the greatest animations ever created, and *When Marnie Was There* is quite possibly their final film, which marks a time I hoped would never come. To say goodbye to Studio Ghibli is to bid farewell to one of the final establishments still practicing old fashioned, hand drawn animation. There's a physicality present in their filmography that no amount of computer trickery can recreate, a tangibility to them that so effortlessly harnesses a quality of grit and realism.

The world truly seems taken over by computers, and today's animated films are no different. This isn't to say that what Pixar has accomplished isn't extraordinary, because it most certainly is. There is however, an inherent innocence injected into the films Studio Ghibli has so tirelessly created, an element of wonder that could only be achieved by pencil lead in fingernails, and cramped hands from excessive coloring. This gleeful, imaginative wonder is overflowing in every second of *When Marnie Was There*, a gorgeous animation about an introverted girl who discovers a magical, abandoned home on the other side of a pond, as well as her first true friend, Marnie. The movie is exploding with eye-popping imagery, yet its real power lies in the heartfelt story of these two girls who need each other in ways they can't possibly imagine. Speaking of the imagery, the decrepit house that rests across the water is sensationally haunting and often sent chills through my body, an uncommon feat for a "family film," although it shouldn't be labeled as such.

There's this curious phenomenon where people get turned off to a film—or any form of culture, really—simply because it's "foreign." I have a good friend who enjoys the majority of animated releases here in America. When I told him I'd seen a great new movie and referred to it as "anime," he immediately replied, "Skip." Please don't make that mistake. Don't let this beautiful film escape your grasp simply because it wasn't created in America. If subtitles really bother you, you can always settle for the English dub. Just see it. If this truly is Studio Ghibli's final film, they went out with an emotional and heart-wrenching bang.

MAD MAX: FURY ROAD (2015)

ACTION | ADVENTURE | SCI-FI

QUICK FACTS

Director:
George Miller

Starring:
Tom Hardy
Charlize Theron
Nicholas Hoult

Studio:
Kennedy Miller Mitchell

Modern action movies have really lost something. When people talk about the best action films ever made, they invariably mention films like *Die Hard* or *The Matrix*. Films that came out last century. Sad, isn't it? Say thanks to George Miller, then, for taking us back to the 80s with *Mad Max: Fury Road*, a wildly inventive thrill machine that never quits.

The original trilogy (also directed by Miller) starred Mel Gibson as the titular Max, a man of few words just trying to survive the wasteland. Kudos to Tom Hardy for slipping nicely into the shoes of Gibson's famous post-apocalyptic scavenger.

But the real star of the *Mad Max* films was always the set pieces. In *Fury Road*, Miller's command of the chase sequences puts today's action to shame. There's an almost constant "how'd-they-do-that?" sense of awe in every scene. One can only hope that this 71-year-old director has many films left in him, because he still directs like he's 25.

Charlize Theron's ass-kicking Furiosa, Max's reluctant ally, warranted much acclaim. Some even claim she's the film's true protagonist. I feel these statements are made by people less versed in *Mad Max* lore. Save for the first film, Max was always the quiet benefactor of some civilization in need, disappearing into the background once his work was done.

Fury Road is the best pure action film so far this decade. The practicality of the stunt-work and the hard-edged performances from Theron and Hardy make *Fury Road* a fast-paced trip worth taking.

CREED (2015)

DRAMA | SPORT

QUICK FACTS

Director:
Ryan Coogler

Starring:
Michael B. Jordan
Sylvester Stallone
Tessa Thompson

Studio:
Chartoff-Winkler
Productions

The first time I saw *Rocky*, I simply didn't get it. I was too naïve to feel its impact. "Where's the action?" I wondered. "This is a boxing movie right?" Wrong. The best *Rocky* films were always dramas at their core—the sports element was simply icing on the cake.

After Sylvester Stallone redeemed the flagging franchise with the surprisingly touching *Rocky Balboa*, I didn't expect to see the charming underdog from Philly on the big screen again. So when news of a spinoff went public, I feared the franchise's legacy might again be tarnished. To my delight, *Creed* is not only a great film but easily the best *Rocky* since the original.

Ryan Coogler (*Fruitvale Station*) directs with such passion for the material, and Michael B. Jordan (playing the late, great Apollo Creed's son Adonis) commits fervently to this shockingly effective film. Yet Stallone's turn as a world-weary *Rocky* nearly steals the show. Tears welled in my eyes on numerous occasions, both from Stallone's heartfelt performance and from Creed's struggle to escape his father's shadow. Stallone and Jordan have marvelous chemistry, and the student-teacher relationship is well-drawn without turning sappy.

I was shaking in my seat, watching that final enthralling match. There wasn't a film in 2015 that affected me so deeply. If you skipped *Creed* for fear it's "just another *Rocky*," you've done yourself a major disservice. Don't miss this film.

STAR WARS: THE FORCE AWAKENS (2015)

ACTION | ADVENTURE | FANTASY

Director:
J.J. Abrams

Starring:
Daisy Ridley
John Boyega
Oscar Isaac

Studio:

Perhaps no film in history was more anticipated than *Star Wars: The Force Awakens*. In fact, that anticipation has led many to unrealistic expectations. The original trilogy is often highly regarded in the minds of fans as untouchable, nearly perfect entertainments. While I do love those films, I also recognize that no film is perfect. In today's day and age, a highly anticipated film that perhaps isn't a work of utter perfection can be lambasted as awful. It's a strange and unwelcome development, but nonetheless, *The Force Awakens* receives a lot of unwarranted hate.

I loved this film, and I honestly feel that in years to come, and especially with future releases, it will garner great respect. Hell, *The Empire Strikes Back* received a surprisingly lukewarm response upon its initial release back in 1980.

The practical creatures, animatronics, and use of real locations and sets make the world feel lived-in and realistic, adding to the grounded and tortured new characters. Kylo Ren in particular, is captivating, enhanced by an impressive performance from Adam Driver. John Boyega is endlessly charismatic as Finn, but the real discovery is Daisy Ridley, who plays one of the best film heroes in recent memory. Her work here is so real that I'm itching to see what else she can do. Another great addition was Oscar Isaac as Poe, a cunning pilot, and a very fun character.

While it follows a similar formula laid out in previous films, *The Force Awakens* also breathes new life into the franchise with its energy, humor, emotion, and above all, characters. It was so refreshing to once again see a *Star Wars* movie with entertaining, likable characters!

It was wonderful seeing Han Solo grace the screen again, and the film wisely makes use of him and the rest of the original cast, teasing us in enticing ways. *The Force Awakens* leaves us wanting more, which is exactly what it should do. Impressive Abrams, most impressive.

Author Bio

Chris Stuckmann has been writing ever since elementary school. What began as short stories scribbled on notepads grew into a serious respect for the craft. His love of filmmaking has led to a successful career in film criticism, and a YouTube channel that has amassed over half a million subscribers.

He lives in Akron, Ohio with his wife, Sam.

Official Website: http://www.chrisstuckmann.com

Foreword by

Winner of the 2014 ICG Publicists Guild Press Award (honoring outstanding entertainment journalism), Scott "Movie" Mantz is the Film Critic and Film Segment Producer for "Access Hollywood." In October 2000, Mantz joined the daily entertainment newsmagazine TV show, which is currently in its 17th season. In addition to his production and celebrity booking duties for "Access Hollywood" and its companion morning show "Access Hollywood Live," Mantz reviews movies on-camera for both shows. Mantz is also a regular contributor to NBC-TV's "The TODAY Show" and is a resident film critic on "Just Seen It," the acclaimed movie review series that airs every week on PBS.

CLOSING

First and foremost, thank you. Without you, I'm not sure where I'd be today. You, kind readers and viewers, have made it possible for me to achieve my dreams. If you ever wondered if I truly cared about you, please know that I do. I'm incredibly grateful for wonderful people like you who share the same passion: the screen.

When I discovered my love for film, I was told by many, many people that my dreams would not be attained. To be completely honest, only my parents seemed to care, largely because they saw the desire in my eyes. And the lack of fulfillment.

When one person told me I required a film degree, three more said not to waste my time. It didn't matter anyway. I barely had $100 to my name when I turned 18 so there was no way I could pay for college. But I continued studying. I watched any film I could get my hands on. No frame went unexamined. Every camera movement documented. I figured that if I couldn't afford school, I was going to devour every piece of film-related information available to me.

Through short-filmmaking, screenwriting and most of all, practice, I learned so much. Now, I must stress that I'm not downgrading the benefits of attending college. What I'm saying is, if you're dirt poor like I was at 18, there are other ways! Don't give up!

Still, to assume that I've learned all there is to know, would be horrifically arrogant of me. When we decide that we've finished learning, we allow ourselves to fail. Maintaining that attitude is important to stay fresh. The moment we look around and say "Well, I guess I'm done now," is the exact moment everything we try to do creatively will suck.

Movies can be truly transformative. They've changed people for the better, inspired them to follow their dreams, even broken cultural barriers. The perfect combination of sound and imagery, with the right touch, can harness something within us that no other art form can. That's why I continue to go to the movies. The screen.

It's my sincerest desire that you've taken something positive away from this book, and even better, that you've discovered a great film you've never seen before. Until next time, have fun at the movies!

- Chris Stuckmann

My Bucket List

- [ ] American Psycho ☆☆☆☆☆
- [ ] Memento ☆☆☆☆☆
- [ ] Unbreakable ☆☆☆☆☆
- [ ] Crouching Tiger, Hidden Dragon ☆☆☆☆☆
- [ ] Spirited Away ☆☆☆☆☆
- [ ] Donnie Darko ☆☆☆☆☆
- [ ] Ocean's Eleven ☆☆☆☆☆
- [ ] Minority Report ☆☆☆☆☆
- [ ] Signs ☆☆☆☆☆
- [ ] X2 ☆☆☆☆☆
- [ ] Pirates of the Caribbean: The Curse of the Black Pearl ☆☆☆☆☆
- [ ] The Last Samurai ☆☆☆☆☆
- [ ] Old Boy ☆☆☆☆☆
- [ ] The Lord of the Rings: The Return of the King ☆☆☆☆☆
- [ ] Spider-Man 2 ☆☆☆☆☆
- [ ] Collateral ☆☆☆☆☆
- [ ] The Incredibles ☆☆☆☆☆
- [ ] Shaun of the Dead ☆☆☆☆☆
- [ ] A History of Violence ☆☆☆☆☆
- [ ] Kiss Kiss Bang Bang ☆☆☆☆☆
- [ ] Caché (Hidden) ☆☆☆☆☆
- [ ] Casino Royale ☆☆☆☆☆
- [ ] The Departed ☆☆☆☆☆
- [ ] The Bourne Ultimatum ☆☆☆☆☆
- [ ] Zodiac ☆☆☆☆☆

☐ There Will Be Blood	☆ ☆ ☆ ☆ ☆
☐ No Country for Old Men	☆ ☆ ☆ ☆ ☆
☐ Trick 'R Treat	☆ ☆ ☆ ☆ ☆
☐ The Dark Knight	☆ ☆ ☆ ☆ ☆
☐ Coraline	☆ ☆ ☆ ☆ ☆
☐ 500 Days of Summer	☆ ☆ ☆ ☆ ☆
☐ Inglourious Basterds	☆ ☆ ☆ ☆ ☆
☐ Inception	☆ ☆ ☆ ☆ ☆
☐ Toy Story 3	☆ ☆ ☆ ☆ ☆
☐ Drive	☆ ☆ ☆ ☆ ☆
☐ Mission Impossible: Ghost Protocol	☆ ☆ ☆ ☆ ☆
☐ The Avengers	☆ ☆ ☆ ☆ ☆
☐ Snowpiercer	☆ ☆ ☆ ☆ ☆
☐ Prisoners	☆ ☆ ☆ ☆ ☆
☐ Captain America: The Winter Soldier	☆ ☆ ☆ ☆ ☆
☐ Enemy	☆ ☆ ☆ ☆ ☆
☐ Under the Skin	☆ ☆ ☆ ☆ ☆
☐ Edge of Tomorrow	☆ ☆ ☆ ☆ ☆
☐ The Babadook	☆ ☆ ☆ ☆ ☆
☐ Birdman	☆ ☆ ☆ ☆ ☆
☐ Whiplash	☆ ☆ ☆ ☆ ☆
☐ When Marnie Was There	☆ ☆ ☆ ☆ ☆
☐ Mad Max: Fury Road	☆ ☆ ☆ ☆ ☆
☐ Creed	☆ ☆ ☆ ☆ ☆
☐ Star Wars: The Force Awakens	☆ ☆ ☆ ☆ ☆

Thank You:

*"A much needed "thank you" goes out to Scott Mantz,
Andy Signore and Jeremy Jahns for their thoughtful words!"*

- Chris Stuckmann

CPSIA information can be obtained at www.ICGtesting.com
Printed in the USA
BVOW11s0716270216

438298BV00002B/2/P